"Arianna Molloy's *Healthy Calling* burnout's darkness. Through her profound insights and practical strategies, Molloy guides readers on a transformative journey from despair to hope, from exhaustion to renewal. This book is essential reading for anyone seeking true fulfillment in their work."

Michael J. Arena, dean of the Crowell School of Business at Biola University and author of Adaptive Space

"By bringing humility to a working world driven by achievement, urgency, and overwhelming demands, Dr. Arianna Molloy reminds her readers of the only satisfaction that can truly last. Dr. Molloy's insightful book *Healthy Calling* offers a timely and powerful reminder that anything that is not God is an idol and that we glorify God best when we rest in him first. Dr. Molloy's refreshingly honest wisdom and informed compassion lead us to a renewed, deeper, and sustainable joy in the good work for our good God that we have each been truly called to do."

Carolyn Weber, professor at New College Franklin, international speaker, and award-winning author of *Surprised by Oxford* and *Holy is the Day*

"Arianna Molloy has done more than write a professional, practical, and personal book on what it means to be truly called to a job and a career, all the while managing the burnout that plagues so many. *Healthy Calling* is an exceptional road map for pursuing your callings in healthy and sustainable ways by developing a dynamic relationship with the Caller. Whether you are a student or a seasoned professional, Dr. Molloy's thoughtful research and experience will provide the confidence you need to live a life of humility and gratitude as you pursue the callings God has given you."

Stan Jantz, CEO of the Come and See Foundation

"It's a beautiful thing to have a calling and not just a career . . . to feel as if every time the paycheck hits your account, you're robbing the bank because it doesn't feel like work. But it's also a dangerous place to be, and don't I know it. When what you do is what you love, it's more than easy to transgress boundaries and freefall into burnout and even shame. What then? In *Healthy Calling*, Dr. Arianna Molloy gives us much needed guidance. This will be a book I return to time and again."

Bryan Loritts, author of *Enduring Friendship* and teaching pastor at the Summit Church

"Arianna Molloy addresses a critical issue few works on calling explore—the danger of allowing passion for work to lead to exhaustion and burnout. As she uncovers the darker side of calling, Molloy steers readers toward biblical insight and practical action that restore a healthier experience of vocation. I wish this book had been written earlier in my career! Highly recommended for anyone flirting with burnout in their current role."

Joanna Meyer, founder and executive director of Women, Work, & Calling

"The culture sugarcoats and oversimplifies work as a calling with 'live your bliss' and 'do what you love' mantras. The truth is far more complex and so much richer. In *Healthy Calling*, Arianna Molloy explores this reality thoughtfully, rigorously, and personally. With deep humility and great clarity, she offers a fresh, grounded, eminently practical perspective on living a calling in the real world. I couldn't put it down, and I can't recommend it highly enough."

Bryan Dik, author of *Redeeming Work* and coauthor of *Make Your Job a Calling*

"*Healthy Calling* is an essential read for our times. Arianna has her finger on the pulse of this cultural moment, offering profound insights into the challenges we face in our work lives today. I found myself reading with a highlighter in hand, marking passage after passage of wisdom. What sets this book apart is how Arianna masterfully blends rigorous academic research with actionable, practical advice. *Healthy Calling* isn't just a guide—it's a lifeline for anyone seeking to transform their work from a source of stress into a sustainable vocation."

Paul Sohn, director of the Center for Faith & Work, author of *Quarter-Life Calling*

ARIANNA
MOLLOY

HEALTHY
CALLING

FROM TOXIC
BURNOUT TO
SUSTAINABLE
WORK

ivp

An imprint of InterVarsity Press
Downers Grove, Illinois

InterVarsity Press
P.O. Box 1400 | Downers Grove, IL 60515-1426
ivpress.com | email@ivpress.com

InterVarsity Press® is the publishing division of InterVarsity Christian Fellowship/USA®. For more information, visit intervarsity.org.

All Scripture quotations, unless otherwise indicated, are taken from The Holy Bible, New International Version®, NIV®. Copyright © 1973, 1978, 1984, 2011 by Biblica, Inc.™ Used by permission of Zondervan. All rights reserved worldwide. www.zondervan.com. The "NIV" and "New International Version" are trademarks registered in the United States Patent and Trademark Office by Biblica, Inc.™

While any stories in this book are true, some names and identifying information may have been changed to protect the privacy of individuals.

The publisher cannot verify the accuracy or functionality of website URLs used in this book beyond the date of publication.

Cover design: David Fassett
Interior design: Daniel van Loon

ISBN 978-1-5140-0840-9 (print) | ISBN 978-1-5140-0841-6 (digital)

Printed in the United States of America ♾

Library of Congress Cataloging-in-Publication Data

Names: Molloy, Arianna, 1981- author.
Title: Healthy calling : from toxic burnout to sustainable work / Arianna
  Molloy.
Description: Downers Grove, IL : IVP, [2025] | Includes bibliographical
  references.
Identifiers: LCCN 2024025119 (print) | LCCN 2024025120 (ebook) | ISBN
  9781514008409 (print) | ISBN 9781514008416 (digital)
Subjects: LCSH: Career development–Philosophy. | Career
  development–Religious aspects Christianity. | Burn out
  (Psychology)–Religious aspects Christianity. | Humility–Religious
  aspects Christianity. | BISAC: RELIGION / Christian Living / Calling &
  Vocation | SELF-HELP / Personal Growth / Success
Classification: LCC HF5549.5.C35 M66 2025 (print) | LCC HF5549.5.C35
  (ebook) | DDC 158.7/23–dc23/eng/20240701
LC record available at https://lccn.loc.gov/2024025119
LC ebook record available at https://lccn.loc.gov/2024025120

31   30   29   28   27   26   25 | 12   11   10   9   8   7   6   5   4   3   2   1

What should I do when the answer might seem obvious but is my genuine thought? I must choose it anyway. So, I dedicate this book to my great Caller. What a gift to know you and be known by you. My Lord, you have faithfully loved me again and again and again. I am yours.

To the ones the Caller has given me, so I may hear his voice and feel his love even more. To my parents, Bill and Johanna; my husband, Allen; and my son, Asher. Thank you for reflecting the Caller's love to me. I know him better because of you.

And, to you, my friend—reader of this book. Thank you for letting me walk beside you in this journey. May the bright light of our Caller shine on you. May you feel the closeness of his warmth guide the way.

CONTENTS

INTRODUCTION

THE PATH TO BURNOUT
AND WHY IT MATTERS

Burnout starts with deception.

My dad is one of the wisest, most humble people I know, and he often describes *deception* as being most powerful in the non-obvious. Think of it this way: deception is like lounging on an inner tube in the water on a sleepy, summertime day. You close your eyes and gently drift along. Then suddenly, you open your eyes and realize you've drifted so far away from the shore that you don't know how to get back.

I know this firsthand.

It was the third year into my job as a full-time professor when I woke up in the middle of the night sweat-soaked, my heart beating like I'd been running instead of sleeping, with my mind alert like it was the middle of the day. This was not the first night such an experience occurred. It was starting to become a pattern.

On this particular night, I began thinking about my recent behavior and interactions: as a communication professor I am trained to focus on what we do and say, and what that means. I mentally checked off the past several weeks, hoping to uncover some reason for this assault on my sleep. Lately, when I'd arrive at work, I would linger in my car longer than normal, mindlessly scrolling social media, photos on my phone, my calendar, or even the Google search bar. Have you ever done that? I just didn't want to get out of the car. I needed every extra minute I could squeeze out. For what? I didn't know.

One afternoon, I was so zoned out that I didn't even notice my friend Sarah coming to knock on the car window. It startled me in a way that could easily fit into a Netflix movie comedy—lecture notes flying all over the dashboard, coffee cup falling over, and me yelping in embarrassment.

She asked with a wry smile, "What are you doing? Are you okay?"

I laughed it off, saying, "Oh yeah, I'm totally fine," got out of the car, and went to work. But I wasn't okay.

What else was going on at that time? I was teaching an overload of classes, on too many university service committees, and recently got engaged and was deep into planning a wedding. Despite all of this, I was also continuing to say yes to more— more opportunities, more tasks to add to my ever-growing list, more people to meet. Why? Partly it was because I finally found a meaningful job and most of the opportunities were ones I actually wanted. I know, this is not a bad problem. But it's still a problem.

Saying yes to good things is often more seductive than saying yes to obviously bad ones. The truth is that I felt *called* to be a professor, specifically to work with college students. I loved it. It brought me joy. And one of the most disorienting kinds of transitions is when something that once brought anchoring joy loses its meaning. We become adrift without realizing it.

So as I lay in bed with the darkness of the night seeping through the cracks of my curtains, with a mind and body reacting like I'd just run a half marathon and a soul withering in thirst, internal red alarms started going off, sounding a warning I couldn't ignore. Here's the thing: I study communication about work as a calling. At its most basic definition, a *calling* is "the experience of feeling a deep compelling or pull toward a particular life pursuit or dedication." My dissertation, publications, and talks all focus on the bright and dark sides of experiencing work as a calling.

The bright side of a work calling is powerful! Research shows that those who identify their work as a calling have greater motivation and overall life satisfaction than their peers, can overcome economic shifts and organizational change better, and are major contributors to healthy and positive work climates.[1] They are *more* resilient and can handle economic and organizational change *better* than their peers. They are willing to stick it out longer when things are hard, and they are often the ones leading others with a sense of perseverance and passion for the work they are doing. So employers want to hire more of these types of people.

I also knew the dark side of calling is dangerous. More than any other peer group at work, those who feel called are also the most prone to workaholism, job idolization, organizational manipulation, and ultimately burnout.[2] I knew these implications of the dark side, but now I was living it. I was burned out.

I recalled my dad's words about deception. Despite all my training, I hadn't seen this coming, because burnout thrives on deception. It is easy to disregard it until there's a physical, mental, and/or spiritual breakdown. Though we often think of burnout as a category, or a neat and tidy, easy-to-spot kind of setback, it's actually more of a spectrum. This is part of the problem. Burnout is rarely felt, seen, or acknowledged until we are almost, or are already, overtaken by it. Burnout often starts with good intentions to strive toward an admirable goal, but it takes over when we've lost sight of the goal within the context of the rest of our lives.

Burnout has become such a ubiquitous term today that we've almost forgotten its meaning or why it's worthwhile to examine. We may even be feeling burned out from the topic of burnout! The problem is, it still matters because it's still rampant. We can't disengage from this topic, but we won't stay here. We have to talk about burnout like traveling through a tunnel; we need to get to the other side, because life is better there. But we have to focus our attention on navigating our way through the tunnel to get to our destination. Although various definitions of burnout are floating around, both academic and popular culture writers agree on a few aspects. Take note about which of the following resonate the most in your own life.

BURNOUT IS ROOTED IN CHRONIC STRESS

In general, burnout is a kind of physical, psychological, emotional, and mental exhaustion. It manifests differently in different people, often including feelings of deep overwhelm, being emotionally drained, and unable to accomplish everyday tasks. It can sound like cynicism masquerading as humor or intelligence; or even toxic positivity instead of authentic listening and compassion. And it is typically brought about by *prolonged* stress.

Now, a few weeks of high stress (launching a new product at work, starting a new job, moving homes, doing your taxes, finals week in college, etc.) can be exhausting and hard, but this isn't the kind of prolonged stress we're talking about here. That type of stress limits our focus to the bare necessities so we can get to the other side. It is meant to be momentary and situational. It's essentially "good stress" in that it helps us push through hard times by creating an extra boost of adrenaline and extreme focus needed to survive. We may get bumps and bruises from it, but we see a clear time when we can stop that pace of living and heal. Good stress is a survival technique, part of our design to give us emergency measures to make it through desperate times or challenging circumstances.

Bad stress, on the other hand, is not momentary: it is chronic. It is living a life defined by stress, without a plan and accountability for change. It is stress that becomes normal to us. We are so used to living a stressful life that any kind of calm or quiet seems concerning and even uncomfortable. So we adjust to this long-term stress, little by little, not realizing how far we are drifting from our goals. Bad stress results in burnout.

THERE'S BURNOUT, AND THEN THERE'S TOXIC BURNOUT

While burnout in general is definitely concerning—leading to depression, anxiety, increased sick days, relational conflict, a kind of psychological paralysis, and an overriding sense of shame[3]—burnout from a calling is more than that; it can be devastating to the core.

When *calling burnout* happens, it includes all of those concerning attributes mentioned above, plus a sense of dissociation with a purpose for living, a kind of spiritual and relational burnout. Because a calling involves some kind of identification with a Caller, when we experience calling burnout, it involves a disconnect with the Caller and surrounding community. Here, a rising sense of shame emerges, and it isn't just about the self. The shame is relational. People who feel general burnout might respond with various levels of "I don't like what I'm *doing* anymore." But people who identify a sense of calling and feel burnout respond more like, "I don't know who I *am* anymore."[4]

The relational obligation that comes with a sense of calling can easily override personal boundaries and healthy parameters. A need is great, and we feel the pull to meet that need. Renowned theologian, author, and Pulitzer Prize winner Frederick Buechner points to *calling* as "the place where your deep gladness and the world's deep hunger meet."[5] This is very moving because it appeals to the visceral sense of calling. But let's not go too fast here. There's a reverent tone in Buechner's words that we tend to skip over.

If we identify with feeling called, it means we sense a significant need that we know we can help fill. The scary part is, if we invert our role in the calling dynamic, if we begin to think of ourselves as the Caller, it's very hard to say no. We are no longer accountable to the Caller because we *are* the caller. The plumb line gets skewed in a kind of moral vertigo based on the magnetic pull of the need we see before us, often letting panic or scarcity guide decision-making.

When we recognize our role as the *called*, we offer up the big picture vision and the important details to an omnipotent, omnipresent, omniscient God who can see the details and the larger scene with a mindset of care, order, and peace.

False control from assuming the role of caller also means we may minimize ethics and integrity for the sake of the goal before us. We may justify ignoring healthy boundaries for the sake of the need we see, adding greater confusion about when and why we might want to say no or not right now. Remember, burnout thrives on deception and our personal dismissal of boundaries.

From the outside, burnout behaviors from a calling look very similar to the pursuit and experience of meaningful work, what psychologist Angela Duckworth describes as *grit* (passion plus perseverance), or even what social innovator Greg McKeown frames as *essentialism* (choosing what is most important and investing wholeheartedly in that endeavor).[6] However, burnout is not the same as grit or essentialism because it does not yield long-term positive results.

Calling burnout has a distinct toxicity. And those of us most prone to burnout are already primed to push ourselves beyond what is healthy, because we are highly motivated, enjoy working toward a goal, and often feel deeply passionate about what we are doing for the sake of others.

Consider the metaphor of burnout: What is left after something is burned out? Ashes. Broken pieces. An unrecognizable shape of something that once was. Perhaps you're feeling that right now. Maybe you've gone from doing something truly meaningful, something you genuinely felt called to do, to now feeling like a fragmented shadow of yourself. Maybe you're somewhere on the border of apathy and emptiness. Maybe you're feeling frozen by a lack of knowing how to move forward because your internal compass feels broken. My friend, you are not alone, and you don't have to stay here in this.

In order to avoid calling burnout, or recover from it if we're already there, we need to understand it a bit better. So we'll peel back the burnout process a little bit. We'll look at how the sausage gets made, and while it should feel uncomfortable, hopefully it will also feel illuminating. We need to turn the lights on.

A NEW BLUEPRINT

How can those of us who feel called pursue work in a healthy way? We've got to establish a new blueprint. Defining and recognizing *calling burnout* is the first step. The second step is knowing what will help mitigate this tendency. The final step is learning how to implement it.

What has emerged from my own research and experience is that there is a particular quality of human emotion and mental focus that is essential to help prevent burnout, and which leads to a healthy calling. Some may call this virtue *humble self-understanding* or *humble discernment*. We'll spend some time unpacking the concept of walking humbly (that ancient rule from Micah 6:8) and working through what it looks like to integrate this practice into our daily life, work, and relationships in a way that sets us up for sustainable, long-term success.[7]

I commit to walking with you through the following layers of emotional whiplash, spiritual labor, and cognitive overload. In part one of this book, we visit the distinct relationship between experiencing a calling and getting to burnout. We explore the

deadly duo of workaholism and job idolization, so we can know
how to recognize and recover from these seductive dynamics. In
part two, we explore the topic of humility as the essential quality
which both helps protect and revive a calling. And in part three,
we focus on the practical ways we can implement humility in life
right now.

When burnout overtakes you, it can feel unbelievably disorienting, even shaming. As you're reading this, you may even feel
doubtful that a change is possible. I cannot promise it will be easy,
quick, or a one-time-fix experience. In fact, I can almost promise
it won't be.

What I can tell you is this: your Caller knows you. He's the best
communicator. He knows what your heart is saying, even if you
can't hear it anymore. You don't have to explain yourself to him
or wonder if he misunderstood you. He hears you. He is coming
for you. A calling involves a *relationship* with the Caller, so you will
need to do some work too. But know this: He has promised to
rescue you, walk with you, and bring you to a spacious place
(Psalm 18:19).

There's a story about a person who fell down a hole. A doctor
walked by and the person shouted from below, "Hey, can you help
me get out?!" The doctor stopped, pulled out a medical pad, scrib-
bled something down, dropped it down the hole, and kept walking. A little while later, a pastor walked past the hole. The person
in the hole shouted, "Hey, can you help me get out?!" The pastor
paused with a bowed head, said a prayer, and kept walking. Then,
a friend walked by and the person in the hole, quite desperate and
exhausted at this point, managed to cry out one more time, "Hey,
can you help me get out?!" The friend stopped, looked down, and
jumped in the hole. The person in the hole was in despair, and
said, "Why did you jump down this hole? Now we are both stuck."

The friend smiled, "I jumped in because I've been down this hole before, and I know the way out."

I've been down this burnout hole before. I want you to know you are not alone. I'm jumping in with you, and I'll walk beside you as we find the way out.

STYLE AND STRUCTURE

Lists and calendar planning are almost a love language for me. In the spirit of seeing structure as a helpful guide, at the end of each chapter I've provided questions for you to consider. Feel free to spend more time on the one or two that grab at your heart and mind—they are for you. They will be especially helpful if you find a space to process them, whether in a journal or with a friend. You'll notice there's also a concluding prayer. Each one I have prayed over you as I wrote this book. May it be a help to you in this calling journey.

One final style note: this book is written from an explicitly Christian perspective. As a communication researcher and teacher, as one who has experienced feeling called, living a calling, being burned out, and coming back from it (more than once), I cannot ignore the lived truth that all I have learned about being a good communicator comes from my relationship with God. I will bring faith into this conversation, not as a forced instrument or a hammer, but rather as an illuminator.

If you're curious about work as a calling, or have been struggling with an intrinsic sense of burnout that goes beyond just disliking what you're doing, but feels more like the dark realm of questioning your purpose, this book is written for you.

If you're beginning to lose hope, or have lost hope, about experiencing truly meaningful work; if your day-to-day tasks feel lackluster and arduous; if you're carrying around a dull ache for something more, this book is written for you.

If you are actively thirsty for a restored, revived work calling; if you are scanning the horizon in search of how to grasp hold of more purposeful work, this book is written for you.

If you've been sensing you can't keep doing what you're doing the way you're doing it or you will burn out; if you are hoping to prevent calling burnout from overtaking you because you feel the creep of burnout getting close, this book is written for you.

If you're questioning who God is in your life, or don't consider yourself a Christian at all, but you care about experiencing healthy, meaningful work, I truly believe there's something here for you.

One of my favorite verses from the Bible is "In your light we see light" (Psalm 36:9). If we are going to talk about burnout, we also need to talk a bit about what brings light. I am suggesting it's in relationship with God. However, if this is not how you identify yourself, I still believe this book is for you. We cover a good amount of peer-reviewed research and lived stories that can benefit and help you.

Let's get started.

PART ONE

THE TERRAIN
OF BURNOUT

THE TOXIC RELATIONSHIP
BETWEEN BURNOUT
AND CALLING

What hat kinds of stories draw your attention?

For me, I love underdog stories. There's something visceral about the way a person identifies a longing, pursues it, and runs into multiple and sometimes massive, seemly insurmountable obstacles. I think to myself, *There's no way this is going to work out*. It's almost too painful to watch but too compelling to look away. Then, usually with the help of others, somehow, the underdog perseveres and reaches their goal. And in the process, they are changed forever.

Living out a calling while avoiding burnout, surviving burnout, or recovering from burnout is the best kind of underdog story.

There is a classic film I love—the true-life story of Eric Liddell, an Olympic gold medalist and subsequent missionary to China. In the movie *Chariots of Fire*, the opening scene follows very white-legged men, charging across a gray beach, in stark white cotton running clothes, while what is now a classic '80s music soundtrack marks the momentum of their run.[1] The camera pans across the faces of each runner. Some faces are marked with varying levels of determination, others have a kind of absent-minded going-through-the-motions look. One guy even carries an expression of fun, like he's at his favorite party. But another young man tilts his head up to the sky with an intimacy typically kept for someone before a deep embrace. This is Eric Liddell.

Liddell is a future missionary and an athlete. Interestingly he has the support from his family to be a missionary but not an Olympic runner. His sister, feeling frustrated, expresses that she doesn't understand why he wants to do both.

At one point, he tries to explain, saying, "God made me for a purpose, but he also made me fast. When I run, I feel his pleasure." In the course of the film Liddell experiences several instances of being misunderstood, ridiculed by his peers, judged unfairly. We see him wrestle with his own boundaries of integrity for what a healthy calling looks like in action. Ultimately, he leans into what he knows to be true and good and right. He runs with his face lifted up to his Caller, and he wins. And even before the big Olympic gold-medal achievement, he finds deep joy in pursuing what he was created to do.

I watch this movie about every three years. One viewing in particular (when I was in graduate school and working part time as a consultant) left a significant impact. At the time, I was feeling really weary and ragged. On the comfort of my small sofa, with my favorite worn blanket, and a bowl of peanut butter and chocolate ice cream in hand, I was struck once again with the layers of hardship Liddell experienced in pursuit of his calling. It wasn't just that, though.

I was also struck by the incredible fulfillment and deep satisfaction Liddell clearly felt in the midst of this challenging pursuit. Personally, I was thinking, *Wow, whatever I dedicate my life to, I want to feel that way about it.* Professionally, I was thinking, *This is fascinating!*

Satisfaction in work is a compelling idea and a longing most of us can identify with to some degree. Feelings of profound satisfaction in a focused activity is what experts term as *flow*. TED talks, research articles, and social media posts circle around this idea of deep satisfaction known as flow.[2] Certainly, calling includes flow; it involves a deep, intrinsic fulfillment. However, they are not the same. We can experience flow alone, but calling is always connected to others. There's an inherent relational bond with our Caller and with the community impacted by our work calling. In some sense, you could say flow is part of calling but calling is so much more than flow.

And that's where we'll start! This first chapter is like the Disney ride Soarin'. We take a bird's-eye-view tour of some important concepts related to calling, and briefly feel the breeze and smell the scents of certain key ideas. Then in the following chapters, we get off the tour and camp out a bit, lingering in spaces that could truly alter our understanding of a healthy calling. But our first step involves looking at a larger umbrella concept: the role and significance of meaningful work.

THE VALUE OF MEANINGFUL WORK

How do we define *work*? In general, work encapsulates anything we spend a significant portion of our physical, mental, and/or emotional effort doing on a regular basis.[3] In contemporary Western society, the average person changes jobs approximately ten times between the ages of eighteen and forty-two.[4] Work makes up more than a third of our adult lives. For good or for bad, much of our community is now found in our professional lives.

The blurred boundaries between professional and personal life are growing even fuzzier. There's a wider acceptance of hybrid and virtual work cultures, and technological advances encourage overwork and reachability at all times of the day. The result? Our time spent working covers a larger landscape of our lives than we realize.

When we talk about meaningful work, it's important to understand that *meaningful work* is a subjective term.[5] What one person finds especially meaningful, another may find arduous or at the very least boring. For example, my mother loves gardening. Not only does she have a green thumb, but her nurturing spirit flourishes when she gardens. In contrast, plants hide from me. I feel truly delighted by their aesthetic, but they don't "talk" to me. I don't know when they are thirsty or if they need more sun. I find gardening laborious and the opposite of meaningful.

Meaningful work is meaningful to the person who does it, but we can experience a tension between what we value and what society deems valuable. The subjectivity of meaningful work is both personal and collective. Some types of work are viewed by our culture as more valuable than others. This is particularly true if the work is high-paying, prestigious, or requires significant office time, as opposed to unpaid positions, "unskilled labor," or pursuits that are seen by others as frivolous or uninteresting.[6] But what others give value to does not inherently make that work valuable.

Let's stop here for a moment. If you've been feeling devalued for the work you're currently doing, which may not seem like important work to others, now is the time to stop apologizing or making yourself small on their account. Mentally and emotionally own what you are doing. If it's meaningful to you, that matters.

Despite how it may seem, a sense of meaningful work is not reserved for certain types of jobs. I've interviewed participants across a wide variety of workplaces, such as CEOs, artists, hair stylists, athletes, stay-at-home parents, lawyers, medical professionals, educators, construction workers, and accountants. Although certainly different types of occupations more easily lend themselves to meaningful work, the data shows it's less about the work and *more about the person* doing the work.[7] The truth is, within each sphere of work there are people who find deep meaning in it. Their stories are powerful.

In my doctorate program, I started pursuing this idea of meaningful work and work as a calling more fully. Immersed in interviews with people from various work roles, I began making note of their stories, and I found consistent themes among those who felt a sense of meaningfulness and calling, regardless of their field. Check this out:

- A hospital performance consultant described their work as "that kind of fire in your belly."
- A dog trainer described what they do as "the type of work that feeds your soul. You wake up in the morning and you're looking forward to doing it and you go to bed at night and you're proud that you did it."
- An acupuncturist specializing in fertility needs stated emphatically, "I don't play the lottery, but if I did, and I won $10 million, I'd be doing this. I love what I do. I feel incredibly, unbelievably blessed."

When work is meaningful, it can be an indication that we've been called to it. So let's dig into the subject of calling.

WHAT'S MISSING IN THE CALLING CONVERSATION?

Calling can certainly be a loaded word. Perhaps others have used the term *calling* well, to explain what compels them. Or, it's been used poorly, selfishly, as an excuse not to show up for others, or even as a form of manipulation to get those who feel called to work. more for less (less pay, less recognition, less health, less help, etc.).

If you've had the idea of calling used in your life in a way that has caused trauma, guilt, shame, or feeling left out, I want to pause and say to you: I'm so sorry. I'm so sorry this concept has been used inappropriately against you. That's not okay. A healthy calling should bring healing, not harm. If you're willing, just for right now, try to separate the word *calling* from the person or persons who used it wrongly.

Let's peel back some of these layers.

While the topic of calling is not new—and amazing scholars and writers have provided key insights into calling—one thing still seems to be missing from the conversation: Calling is inherently about communication. Calling is not a static thing. It is not something that happens once, in a contained way.

Calling is about communication between the called, the Caller, and community. I'm not saying this just because communication is my area of study. To have a calling necessarily implies that someone or some thing is calling us. As Christians, we know the Caller is God.[8] We also know that our great call, coming from the greatest command, is to love God and to love others (Matthew 22:37-40). As followers of Christ, our primary calling to love God is reflected in how we love others. In this way, calling is not just about the Caller and the called, it is also about the community we impact, and by whom we are impacted.

Calling is a dynamic relationship between the Caller, the called, and the community. And like any relationship, our calling is ever-developing. Until we recognize calling is about *relationship*, about actual interaction, we miss the entire point of the calling experience.

Like any relationship, which involves ongoing communication, understanding calling as a *communicative process* is key. At its very core, work calling indicates an ongoing visceral interaction between a Caller and the one being called.

New York Times best-selling author, pastor, teacher, writer, and podcast host John Mark Comer reminds us that to be human means we change, grow, and develop. And this, he says, "is by God's design."[9] If part of the human experience is continual growth, straddling an invisible line between being (who we are now) and becoming (who we will be), then our relationship with the Caller is also meant to be dynamic. This means that what you're going through right now has the potential to inform your calling.

So much unseen work goes into the formation and development of a calling, like the underwater part of an iceberg. I remember going on an Alaskan cruise and witnessing the almost unearthly beauty of icebergs. In the frosty, early mornings they seemed to have a faint glow in the water. It was literally breathtaking. What's shocking is we see only the tip. What we don't see, what's below, is the majority.

The formation and development of calling is like an iceberg. A considerable amount of the process is below the surface. This matters because the work we do, the work that feels like a calling, may not always be seen by others. It may not always be measurable. The emotional and spiritual labor that we experience may not be fully valued or understood. Others may ask more of us (or we may demand more of ourselves), not realizing just how much we are already giving.

If a missing emphasis on the topic of calling is the relational core, another gap is the privileging of a moment over a journey. While some of us know very early on what our calling is, some don't. And that's completely normal. In fact, it's very common. That's why thinking about work calling as a journey, rather than merely a fixed moment in time, is more accurate.

There's this mythic idea of calling, that it will fall upon you in bright golden rays from heaven, with a loud voice calling out your name. We certainly might have crystal clear epiphany moments, but they aren't isolated. They are connected to a larger story, to other pieces of the puzzle. We need to pay attention to the little things.

Stephen, a financial advisor, described his process of identifying his work calling as both a journey and an epiphany. Originally going to school to become a licensed minister, on his days off he'd constantly gravitate toward reading financial books. At one point in the interview, he said, "And then it dawned on me, they [the books he was reading] were all on the stock market and, I heard God say, not in an audible voice, but in my spirit, 'Why are you denying who you are?'"

We need to pay attention to what we are drawn toward, and look for ways this might be integrated into our calling. It's good to listen and look for those moments of feeling called. The trick is that in the actual moment, we don't often see the larger implications. It isn't until we look back, until we see our story unfolded, that the patterns emerge.

Placing a value on the communication within a calling means the outcome isn't the only concern. There's great value in the process, formation, development, and relationship of calling, in *how* we seek to live out our calling in the everyday. In fact, the apostle Paul gives this charge: "Make a careful exploration of who you are and the work you have been given, and then sink yourself into that" (Galatians 6:4 MSG). When we recognize that calling is not a one-time thing but rather an ongoing process, it means that what we're doing now has the potential to be part of that process. Even if we're in a place of burnout right now, this can help inform our calling if we let it.

THE SWEET SPOT OF WORK AS A CALLING

When we address work as a specific type of calling, it's helpful to unpack a few more aspects of what calling means. As Christians, we have a general calling: to love God and love others. Author and social critic Os Guinness talks about it this way: "Calling is the truth that God calls us to himself so decisively that everything we are, everything we do, everything we have is invested with a special devotion and dynamism lived out as a *response* to his summons and service."[10] He suggests that calling is a kind of responsibility or stewardship that we enact by cultivating particular qualities God has planted in us.

Each of us can live out our calling in ways that bring a deep sense of purpose and meaning. Scholars often distinguish these as *general* and *specific* callings.

While our general calling is to love God and love others, our specific callings are areas in our lives that feel like "sweet spots." Here, our particular skills and passions are used in ways that feel true to the core of who we are, like we are honoring who God made us to be, for the sake of who God is.

What I am intrigued by, and what my research focuses on, is the way we experience work as a *specific* calling. As we talk about work, this includes both paid and unpaid endeavors that we dedicate a large portion of our physical, mental, and/or emotional effort toward doing on a regular basis.

Work could include being a college student, stay-at-home parent, grandparent, or caregiver; intern, artist, performer, athlete, or pastor; seasonal worker or contract worker, contributor to a new start-up company, self-employed, president of a company, and so on. Remember, if you are dedicating a significant portion of your physical, mental, and/or emotional effort toward something on a regular basis, for our purposes in this conversation, that is work.

In general, *work* is typically categorized in three areas: job, career, and calling.[11] A *job* is typically paid work, primarily motivated by a paycheck. The reward is making it to the weekend (e.g., not having to do the job). It does not necessarily involve degree-specific skill sets or passions. It may or may not utilize previous training (college degree, or other work experiences). A job may allow you to pursue other non-paid work that is meaningful, which has a different kind of incentive. The key here is a job does not require or inspire much motivation apart from doing the tasks you've been given because you have to.

A second way to think about work is as a *career*. A career does involve skill sets and passion. It is primarily motivated by upward mobility and explicit rewards (e.g., a promotion, a bigger office, the ability to take a vacation). A career might start off as an intern or baseline position, but there's clear future and growth opportunities. The focus is on how this work allows for professional advancement. There is also a sense of enjoyment at the work being done, but it's motivated by accomplishment.

A *calling* is different. A calling in work is more than just a paycheck, and more than performance and job advancement. It involves four key components: First, an overarching sense of *meaningfulness* in our work—it is work that goes beyond the functional. Second, work calling includes some kind of *caller*. As Christians, we know that the Caller is the Lord (e.g., "My sheep listen to my voice," John 10:27). Third, work calling involves the integration of the individual's *passion and skillset*. One CEO I interviewed said, "Passion is not enough. Passion alone produces a great fan. Passion and skill set produces a great worker."[12] The integration of these two attributes—passion and skillset—addresses the need to be proactive about seeking training and development in the area of calling. For example, a person called to medicine doesn't just walk into the operating room on day one; they need sharpened skills, intentional training, and sufficient experience. Lastly, a work calling involves positively *contributing to society*. In this way, calling is not simply for ourselves; it connects us to others, to community in some manner. Researchers call this *prosocial behavior*.

Now, these categories (job, career, calling) are not distinct types. Sometimes, a person can experience all three aspects in the same work, depending on the season of life. Others may choose a job (something that pays the bills) and also pursue additional work that feels like a calling (which could be an additional paycheck or unpaid work). We might feel like 80 percent of our work is directly connected to a sense of calling, and 20 percent is just a job. It might also feel like the opposite, where 80 percent feels like a job and 20 percent feels like a calling.

Work calling is not simply about paid work. Right now, your work calling could involve being a student, starting your own company, working as an intern, working seasonally or on commission. Your work calling may be as a full-time parent or caregiver. Work calling includes whatever you perceive as a priority focus, dedicate a majority of your time doing, and feel called to. And what you're learning right now, at this particular moment, could very well be an intentional opportunity to sharpen your skills and clarify your passions.

More than just a process and a journey, it is important to recognize that experiencing work as a calling is a privilege. Not everyone gets the same opportunities to pursue their work calling. In an interview with Nancy, a Gallup consultant, she said, "There's plenty of people that just need a job. It's a privilege to be able to live in the realm of calling." Why doesn't everyone experience this privilege in the same way? This is a big, important question with complex answers, and it deserves more space than we have here. But certainly issues like race, gender, socioeconomic status, and environment play a part.[13]

The reality is that not everyone gets the same opportunities, or has the support to pursue their calling so easily. Different cultures place different values and interpretations on work calling. Recent research examines how first generation and second-generation immigrants experience work calling from a unique perspective, tied to the familial responsibilities of surviving and thriving in a new country. There are also multiple callings, like feeling called to a particular kind of paid work and also called to be a parent or a spouse. Multiple callings add depth and beauty to life, but also greater complexity, more complicated responsibility, and sacrifice.

Why does it matter that calling is a process, that it involves continual development, and that not everyone has the same ability or opportunity to experience calling in work? Too often we confuse a calling with a particular title (psychologist, pastor, parent, mentor, student) when we should see it as a combination of skill sets and passions that can be applied to a number of different occupations. In this way, our specific calling is always tied to, and should rest under, our general calling.

In my work with college students, I see them constantly struggling to find "the" occupation—specific work that will give them a sense of security, identity, and legitimacy. I see them carry the worries of their families, the constraints of various societal struggles, and an overwhelming uncertainty that can feel unending. In some sense, there's nothing wrong with wanting clarity of purpose. What can be dangerous is when we place all our identity and worth in this one job; work roles will come and go. Our calling is not confined to one type of occupation.

A little while ago, I was at a weekend BBQ, talking with my friend Evelyn, a fortysomething mother of two, who survived a very scary and long season of cancer. Prior to her diagnosis, she was a therapist. However, after the trauma of her cancer experience (which included several surgeries, chemo, radiation, and major life changes), she realized she couldn't sit in a room all day, listening to the burdens of others. It just wasn't good for her well-being.

As Evelyn was setting up the food, she shyly shared that she'd gotten into real estate. I responded with, "Oh, that's wonderful! And with your counseling background, you'll be so good at that."

She paused, looking rather shocked. "I'd never thought of that. I actually felt ashamed I couldn't handle being a therapist anymore. And for a while now I've wanted to pursue real estate but was embarrassed by what others might think. And I felt guilty that I wouldn't be applying my degree."

I reaffirmed that I thought her background in psychology would give her an incredible advantage in her new profession. She'd still be using her skill set and the passions that ignite her, just in a different way.

The next morning, I received a text from her: "I wanted to thank you for your words of encouragement yesterday. I appreciate you saying that we can apply our skills (God-given) to many different jobs and it isn't the job that defines our skills. That's so empowering and releases so much shame and unnecessary pressure!"

Like any relationship, calling can shift and change in seasons of our life. The Caller doesn't change, but the way we enact with our calling might. Here's what that means: your calling process is your own. Don't let anyone belittle your boundaries or your dreams. Yes, you might need to grow, but others don't know your process, you do. Find wise counsel from those you value and know well, whose lives you want to learn from.

We know meaningful work makes a big difference in satisfaction, motivation, and overall well-being. We know the definition of calling has four layers (meaningfulness, connection with a caller, a combination of skill sets plus passion, and positive community impact). The next step is to understand the specific bright (good) sides of calling and the dark (dangerous) versions of calling.

THE DARK SIDE OF CALLING

Over the past two decades, the concept of work as a calling has been gaining traction in the scholarly world, specifically in vocational psychology and organizational communication. What researchers have determined is that those who feel called in their work experience several positive outcomes. The findings include being more highly motivated in the work they do, having greater overall life satisfaction and well-being, possessing an ability to withstand organizational change, and being a great contributor to the overall work climate for everyone.[14] This is what is called the bright side. We unpack these beautiful attributes in chapter three.

But we need to address the dark side to calling—the hard, often ignored, in the shadows side. Those who feel called are more likely to work overtime, or agree to take on extra responsibilities, without extra pay or acknowledgment. And while there might be some kind of romantic notion about serving, here is where the caution light should start blinking. The seduction of service makes it hard to know where to draw the line between what we *can* do, and what we *should* do. It feels good to be needed, to be wanted, to have a sense of purpose. However, this sense of being compelled and needed, if left unchecked, can lead to workaholism, job idolization, and ultimately burnout.[15]

In the introduction, we talked about *burnout* as a kind of physical, psychological, emotional, mental, and spiritual exhaustion typically brought about by prolonged stress. I was recently talking to a dear friend about my research on burnout. He said, "Okay, I know the data about burnout, but how can you tell if someone is really in burnout? What are some things they'd say? What do they sound like?" It's a good question, as those of us who experience calling burnout are often prone to talk in similar ways or express similar feelings.

Here's the short answer: burnout often sounds like cynicism, dark humor, or toxic positivity (*toxic positivity* is often characterized by palliative responding without thinking, being too quick in our positive responses). Now, just because someone communicates with these features, it doesn't mean they are burned out. But burnout often uses the fake fuel of cynicism.

Let's distinguish between cynicism and critical thinking. *Critical thinking* is good, productive, valuable, and biblical. *Cynicism* is destructive, unhelpful, and the opposite of the fruit of the Spirit.

Cynicism isn't really dialogue, it's monologue. We think we're being smart, but we're really just letting our wounds lead us. Those employing cynicism may use deflection to point at others or dark humor to point at themselves in a way that normalizes the unhealthy behavior as quirky or "that's just me." It does not allow for real self-examination.

Cynicism is easy; vulnerability is hard. Toxic positivity is easy; critical thinking is hard. Ultimately, these unhealthy practices prevent us from changing course and instead can lead deeper into burnout.

BURNOUT AS A MANAGEABLE PROBLEM, NOT A FIXABLE ONE

If those who feel called are also most likely to experience burnout, and if burnout leads to paralyzing mind, body, and soul exhaustion, how can we fix the problem? Well, I've got some good news and some bad news. The bad news is that burnout is *not* a fixable problem. But wait, let's not despair! Burnout is not a fixable problem, but it is a manageable problem. This distinction is key.

As a professor, I talk about the idea of *fixable* and *manageable* problems with my students. A fixable problem is when a light bulb burns out. What do we do? We typically stop what we're doing and replace it. Problem solved. A manageable problem is one that, no matter how hard we try, won't totally go away. It requires adjusting and managing for the long term.

Here's an example: I am blessed to have been raised by two different, but equally loving, parents. My dad is an incredibly considerate person who loves routine and structure. In his mind, being on time is being five minutes early. My mom, on the other hand, despite being one of the most thoughtful people I know, will admittedly tell you that she was not born with a sense of time. My parents have a truly admirable marriage, and their relationship with each other has taught me more about God's love than almost anything else. However, as a kid, a certain kind of tension would start to surface about getting to church on time on most Sundays. I can still feel the stress rising just thinking about it. My dad was ready to go five minutes early, waiting by our front door, keys in hand. My mom was often still fixing her coffee or taking out curlers in her hair—sincerely trying, but not ready.

Eventually, they realized the routine Sunday morning goal of getting to church on time just wasn't working. So they sat down at the kitchen table and figured out a solution. If everyone was ready to go at a certain time, we'd drive together. If my mom needed more time, she'd drive separately. This was a manageable problem because they both realized being on time will always be a top priority for my dad and being on time may be a continual challenge for my mom.

Fixable problems and manageable problems require different focus and different energy. Why? If we can fix it, we focus all of our attention on it because there is an end. If it is manageable, we have to know how much time to spend on it and plan for a long-term awareness.

For those of us who identify with a calling, burnout is not a fixable problem; it is a manageable problem.

This distinction does not need to be discouraging. When we know how to approach burnout, we can locate productive strategies to manage it. In chapter two, we linger in the terrain of burnout a bit longer, so we can understand the terrain and you can know the way out.

It takes courage and vulnerability to learn the rhythms of a healthy calling and the process of keeping burnout at bay. So as you're wading your way through this process, don't wait to get to the other side. Right now, carve out some time to sit down, be still, and listen. If you can, try doing this right now. It's not always obvious, but the Caller is always communicating with us!

I want to speak to one thing directly right now, before we conclude this chapter. A key aspect of burnout, particularly burnout from a calling, is a deep and silencing sense of shame—shame of what other people will think, shame about what your old self thinks, shame about what you missed or lost or failed at doing. If you are feeling shame about being burned out, my friend, you do not need to carry this burden.

Shame is a liar. It is likely lying to you right now. Yet Jesus is described in the Gospel of John as "the light [that] shines in the darkness, and the darkness can never extinguish it" (John 1:5 NLT). Read that again. Notice that it doesn't say the light is separate *from* the dark; it says the light actually shines *in* the dark. Shame tries to turn the lights off and create total darkness, to get you to believe that darkness is normal, that burnout is normal.

Jesus is the light who shines in the darkness. His light doesn't have to wait for the darkness to leave, it overrides it. His light shines in the darkness. Burnout is not the end. Burnout is not your life story.

GUIDING QUESTIONS

1. Think about your own work, the work you're doing right now. How do you tend to approach it?

   • What's your mindset about work these days?

   • What's your heart attitude? I recently realized I was telling my young son, "I *have to* go to work." Once I heard myself say this, I changed it to, "I *get to* go to work." The shift in these words is like a compass, moving the needle. Where's your compass pointing these days?

2. When you think of the word *calling*, what comes to mind? Is the term *calling* a word that inspires you, or triggers you?

   - Why do you think that is?
   - Where does this come from?

3. Do you tend to apply the idea of calling to a certain part of your life, or life as a whole?

   - Why do you think that is?

4. Just as burnout is not a category (not easily compartmentalized) but a continuum (more of a range or spectrum), healthy calling is also best thought of as a continuum. Knowing this, the question to consider is no longer: Is your calling healthy or not? Instead, think through how you might answer questions like the following:

   - What practices are you engaging in right now that are helping your calling?
   - What practices are you engaging in that are not helping you?
   - What change can you make this week?

ORIENTING PRAYER

Lord Jesus, you are good. Everything else orients around that truth. When everything else feels confusing, I rest in the knowledge that your goodness is not dependent on my current circumstances. Thank you for the opportunities you've given me. Help me to see the ones I'm missing. Help me to distinguish between opportunity and distraction. Thank you for the passions you've placed in my heart. Please take away the fear that lingers as I look ahead. I need your wisdom and your favor in knowing how to deal with what's in front of me. Help me know when to say yes, and when to say no. Please wipe away the shame of burnout, and show me the way out. Create in me a fresh heart. Amen.

TWO

CHRONIC STRESS AND THE DEADLY DUO OF WORKAHOLISM AND JOB IDOLIZATION

A few years ago my husband, Allen, and I were traveling in Europe for about a week. He completed his graduate work in Oxford, and his class was having a reunion. So we decided to make a fun, quick trip.

Our first night in Oxford we booked a very small room at a hotel called *Malmasion*—literally called "the bad house" in French—which used to be a prison. It was creepy, weird, and interesting. A one-time experience, but an experience nonetheless.

We consumed traditional English breakfast at a parsonage-turned-local-eatery. (I did pass on black pudding. If you don't know what this is, take a moment and look it up.) We lingered at the Eagle and Child pub, also known as the Bird and the Baby, where my C. S. Lewis fangirl heart felt exhilarated at the idea of overlapping a moment with the great author himself.

During this time, we were also training for my first marathon. Allen and I actually fell in love while he helped me learn how to train for races. You can learn quite a lot about someone when they are good at something and you are terrible. Allen was patient and kind throughout my running learning curve. He saw me at my very worst and still spoke goodness over me, going as slow as I needed up the pavement hills and staying by my side as I crossed seemingly impossible finish lines.

On the second day of our UK trip, we ran through the Oxford colleges—the goal was eleven miles. I'd only started running 5K, 10K, and half marathons less than two years before, but I was hopeful to go the distance (yes, I did make that joke). So after stretching, and running through cobblestone alleyways, we made it to the plush layers of green pasture. It filled my lungs with more than just oxygen. I felt alive! My feet were landing on the same paths as literary greats, like J. R. R. Tolkien. As my imagination took hold and traveled to the works of Jane Austen, my eyes scanned the horizon, just in case I actually did see Mr. Darcy and Elizabeth walking through the morning mist.

Because we were trying to fit in as much as possible on this short trip, right after our run—not even showering, in serious runner mode—we rushed to a bus that took us to London, then immediately took the Chunnel to Paris. The Chunnel, or Channel Tunnel, is an undersea tunnel that connects southern England to the northern part of France. I've *heard* it's pretty cool. I still don't know, because as soon as we got to our seats, we both promptly fell asleep. Allen woke up and had to look at which side of the street the cars were driving on to see where we were in the journey.

The next morning, with the intention of visiting the famous artist Monet's home in the afternoon, we had the goal of taking a quick two-to-three-mile run down the famous Champs-Élysées to the Arc de Triomphe. This stretch of land is often referred to as "the most beautiful avenue in the world." So why miss it? We could fit it in . . . right?

Here's the thing, though: I woke up really, really tired and stiff. My body was talking to me, but I ignored it. We were late in our planned schedule, so I only mildly and very briefly stretched. My calves felt extra tight, but I ignored it. I flashed back to a quote

I'd seen on gym walls and homemade signs held up by those cheering on the sidelines: "Pain is weakness leaving the body." I took a quick swig of water and started running. I wanted to do this. I wanted to train, I wanted to push myself, and I wanted to run down the streets of Paris. I felt alive . . . tired, but alive.

Within a few minutes, I felt a pop in my calf, followed by excruciating pain. Turns out, I tore some ligaments. I foolishly tried to ignore it during the rest of the trip, which of course didn't work. Throughout the year-long healing process, I saw four orthopedic doctors and had lots of physical therapy. During this time I kept thinking, *If only I'd listened to my body*. There were so many moments before the actual injury when I could have done something differently. There were so many small choices I could have changed, which may have led to a different outcome. But hindsight's highlighter doesn't acknowledge the dimly lit reality of the moment. We have to pay attention to the whispers.

LET'S HEAR IT FOR THE BODY

What if we stopped believing that old athletic mantra "pain is weakness leaving the body"? What if we honored the way our bodies communicate with us? What if we said, "When my body is crying out, I will listen to it"? This is not the same thing as letting our bodies dictate our thinking or our actions. The body's response doesn't have to be the ultimate authority, nor should it. But completely ignoring and disregarding body signals have substantial repercussions, especially as they relate to burnout.[1]

What if I had given myself a moment on that UK trip to listen to my body? I probably would have heard the following: *I need a break. I need to slow down. I just need a moment, a day, to catch my breath.* Would that have been the end of the world, if I skipped or postponed the next run? No. In fact, had I slowed down enough, I might have realized how tired my body really was. I might have avoided an injury that continues to impact me. I might have been able to make course corrections so I would be able to run the marathon after all.

Our bodies are telling us things. Our bodies are not the boss of us, nor are they irrelevant. Due to physical disability, injury, age, or social constraints, some of us don't always get to choose what our bodies are able to do. But when it is possible, we should aim to live an integrative life, where we pay attention to what's going on in our physical selves and recognize that our mental, emotional, and spiritual states are also deeply connected to our physical state.

In communication theory, the concept that our nonverbal behavior and internal thought processes impact our ideas and actions is called *intrapersonal communication*. While *inter*personal communication is communication with others, *intra*personal communication is communication with ourselves.

As they relate to the quality of our lives, both interpersonal and intrapersonal communication matter! For example, with intrapersonal communication, when we are hunched over, physically curling inward, perhaps scrolling on our phones with our faces and bodies pointing downward, this impacts how we feel, and what we think. Research shows it can in fact make us feel less confident, more tired, and even more self-conscious. When we take up more space, stand, or sit up straight, when we lift up our faces to take in the world around us, this also impacts our emotional and mental state. This same research reveals that confident body posture actually makes us feel more confident, more awake, and more sure of ourselves.[2]

So on a day when we're feeling really bad, sometimes that favorite pair of sweat pants and our favorite ice cream may be what we need. Most of the time, however, taking a shower, eating something healthy, and dressing in clothes we'd normally wear to make a good first impression, even if no one else sees us, can make us feel better and help reframe our thinking. And knowing what choices we can control is part of the process of perseverance.

There is merit in knowing how to push ourselves, to grow. Angela Duckworth's best-selling book *Grit* is a wonderful source for understanding the healthy and beneficial approach of leading with perseverance and passion. But too often we confuse perseverance and passion with something else: a toxic combination of denial and compulsion.

When it comes to caring for our calling, to protecting our calling from being overcome by burnout, we need to understand what it means to listen to our bodies as we push ourselves. We need to recognize the moments when we're ignoring or devaluing our body's response in a stretching or accelerated situation.

DISTINGUISHING BETWEEN DENIAL AND PERSEVERANCE

Here is where the difference between perseverance and denial are key. *Perseverance* is continued effort toward a goal with the ability to modify or adapt if the reward is delayed or an obstacle appears. *Denial* is the refusal to accept limitations and a disdain toward course correction or alteration. In this way, perseverance partners with rest for the sake of long-term goals, while denial is uncompromisingly fixated on short-term goals.

Let's go back to my story and apply these two mindsets. What would perseverance have looked like in my running story? After that long run in the Oxford countryside, and the way my body was reacting, a perseverance mindset would have evaluated the cost of pushing my body too hard, realized the risk to the long-term goal, and said, *You know, I think I need to take a day or two to slow down. Let's go for a gentle walk today and see how I'm feeling tomorrow.* Instead, I took on a denial attitude and said to my body,

I'm not listening to you. You are weak and my will is strong. I'm going to push you because I want what I want now. I didn't realize that I was choosing denial. I thought I was being tough, disciplined.

You want to know a few other words for various types of denial? Denial, if left unchecked, can be a type of compulsion toward something or someone that leads to greater unhealth or even harm, a long-term bad habit that corrodes appropriate boundaries. In the extreme, this is called *addiction*. Another way to think about extreme versions of denial is a having a god-complex, otherwise known as *idolatry* (worship or reverence for what is not divine, what is not God; godlike status we assign to other people or things). Here, the role of pride takes over and we can't see the important limitations actually designed to keep us safe.

Even the word *limitation* typically has a negative taint to it. Yet, a limitation is another way of understanding our boundary lines. Finding a healthy rhythm in life is not about cramming everything we can into every moment. It is not, in fact, about always pushing ourselves past our limits. Yes, good growth often includes being open to getting stretched, to saying yes, when fear tells us to say no. However, more often with a healthy calling, it is essential to say no to some important and good commitments. Why? Because our actual calling and relationship with the Caller merits this kind of protection. But it's rarely fun or pleasant to say no to good things. It often feels bad.

There's a concern of missing out, losing an opportunity, or letting someone down. I remember sharing this concern with a mentor of mine. She nodded her head, and then leaned forward and said, "Yes, but don't confuse the bad feeling of saying no with an actual bad thing." What does that mean? It means limitations might feel restricting in the moment, but knowing our actual limitations is part of remembering we are human. It's part of maintaining perspective.

When we believe limitations are only bad, or saying no means missing out and losing, we risk losing foundational perspective. When we begin to convince ourselves boundary neglect is not the end of the world, and we find ourselves saying "just this once" again . . . and again . . . and again, we risk breaking ourselves. We risk burning out.

That's the thing about burnout. I don't know anyone, ever, who has welcomed burnout. I don't know anyone who wanted to get to burnout. What I do hear is people confusing "pushing through" with "ignoring the signs." Yes, there are times we do need to push through, but make no mistake: burnout is a liar.

We need consistent times of rest and reflection to determine when the lies are approaching. Because the road to burnout is cluttered with well-intentioned mindsets and actions, which at first glance look like perseverance and commitment. Upon greater reflection, they are really a form of addiction or idolization.

CHRONIC STRESS AND THE GENESIS OF BURNOUT

The genesis of burnout is chronic stress. We throw the word *stress* around like we throw dirty clothes into the laundry bin, unthinking and often. Stress itself is not necessarily bad. We can experience good stress with positive or new situations like starting a new job, a new romantic relationship, and so on. Stress can surface from caring deeply about the outcome of an event or situation.

The problem with stress is that we can normalize it to such a degree that we don't see the imminent danger of continual, long-term stress as anything other than an annoyance. This is called chronic stress, or sustained stress. It involves more than temporary mental, physical, psychological, emotional, or spiritual pressure. The internal ramifications are significant, and the

implications of sustained stress on communication and relationships can be startling.

What are some of the consequences of chronic stress on our
communication? Research tells us that sustained stress significantly impacts how we communicate with others and how we
interpret other people's communication with us. The three
ways this is especially evident is in withdrawal, reduced awareness, and physical tension.[3] Let's unpack each one of these and
as we do, if you're willing, try to assess where you are in each of
these categories.

First, when we have chronic stress, we *withdraw*. We avoid and
seek escape. While some elements of withdrawal can be healthy
(it's actually part of the survival mechanism), if we don't recognize and communicate that we need to withdraw for a bit, it can
cause substantial damage to our relationships and work.

Here's a classic example of unhealthy communicative withdrawal: You and your friend are in the car. You're driving and
your friend is sitting in the passenger seat, clearly upset. You
inquire, "Hey, are you okay? Is everything alright?" Your friend
turns their knees away from you, crosses their arms against
their chest, and looks out the window, saying, "I'm fine." That's
nonverbal withdrawal.

Another ubiquitous form of withdrawal is using our phones as
a type of avoidance, because they appear to be a socially acceptable form of perceived focus: meaning we look busy even if we are
mindlessly scrolling the newest cat video. But if we choose to disengage our connection and awareness with those around us, and
stare at the glow of a tiny screen, we are doing what the ostrich
is known for doing—sticking our heads in the proverbial technological sand and thinking no one can see us.

Withdrawal during interaction is typically a response to anxiety. Although very culturally and context dependent, eye contact

is what nonverbal communication researcher, Andersen, says is an invitation to communicate.[4] When we avoid eye contact, this conveys a desire to hide. Remember, it can be a very good thing to remove yourself, to withdraw for rest and recovery. The key is to be aware that you're doing it and to communicate this need.

The second consequence of chronic stress on our communication is *reduced awareness*. When we are in a season of sustained stress, our ability to recognize other people's social cues gets diminished. We are literally unaware of social and environmental signals around us. Have you ever had that experience when you're trying to end a conversation with someone who keeps talking, and you try to politely step back, but they actually step forward and keep talking?

Sustained stress literally blocks our ability to see and interpret relevant social information. This perpetuates a cycle of increased confusion and anxiety.

Reduced awareness as a survival technique is meant to help us focus on "getting through" and only noticing what's absolutely necessary. But as we know, surviving isn't the same as thriving. Surviving isn't even the same as maintaining or doing fine; it's the bare minimum. Like horse blinders or walking around without your glasses or contacts, when we're in seasons of sustained stress we can't see well. We can't see really important things, scenarios, or people well and that will get us into trouble.

The other interesting aspect of reduced awareness is that as we miss the social and environmental cues, we also become overly self-focused—hyperconscious of ourselves in a way that's distracting and distorted. Those with reduced awareness are cognitively overloaded and emotionally fried.

Lastly, the consequence of chronic stress on our communication is evident in immense *physical tension*, manifested in physical and psychological reactions that further cloud healthy communication. This includes the simultaneous impact of increased anxiety, which limits blood flow to the brain, causing negative, confusing messages to those we are interacting with, and even ourselves. Physically, we might experience an increase in heart rate and rapid breathing, cold or sweaty hands, feet jiggling or clenched hands, even a shift in our vocal pitch. Remember, our bodies are signaling us with important messages.

While stress seems to be part of life, chronic stress isn't something to ignore. We need to stay alert to moments that stretch on and turn into seasons, which turn into lifestyles. We must protect our calling from being choked by this deceptive force.

In the pursuit of work as a calling, there will be setbacks. Maybe you're feeling that right now. I've certainly been there. Maybe you're a recent college graduate trying to find a starting job that leads to a sense of calling and you have no idea how to start that process; or you're in mid-career and realizing that your current work has lost its meaning, and feelings of disorientation are taking over; or you've found yourself in a season where really hard life stuff is morphing your work calling into a shell of what it once was. Where can you go from here?

At the start we need to acknowledge the setbacks, the weary muscles, or any part of the pace of life that isn't working anymore. Similarly, if our primary job right now is harder to quantify, harder to explain because it's creative, seasonal, or relational, paying attention to our body in this process matters; it is no less valuable. And whether we like it or not, work cannot be completely compartmentalized from the rest of our lives. So even when the hard seasons aren't happening to us personally but to someone we love, it can take a significant toll on our own work calling.

When the work we have before us enters into a long-term season of stress, we need to pay attention to the flashing lights and pull over, or we will unknowingly enter the dangerous terrain of chronic stress.

THE DEADLY DUO

Taking stock of how chronic stress is impacting us is the first step. But it's not enough. If we truly want to know how to care for our callings well, if we truly want to learn how we might not be overcome by burnout, we need to dig deeper and know the signs!

We need to understand the deadly duo of workaholism and job idolization, and how these two destructive forces can push us over the edge into burnout. Workaholism and job idolization are not the only causes of burnout. Sometimes the unavoidable burdens come from external sources truly beyond our control. It may be that work leadership or work culture has grown toxic. It could be that long-term socioeconomic crises or personal health, family dynamics, or life challenges have taken such a toll that our work calling feels like formless ash rather than a bright light.

Burnout can happen when we feel consistently unsupported, mistreated, marginalized, and/or manipulated so that we ignore our own boundaries. We address some of these challenges in the coming chapters. Our goal right now is to uncover two habits we do have control over and consider how they might need to change.

As a communication researcher, I'm particularly intrigued by how burnout starts to manifest in the ways we interact with ourselves and with others. Are there hints in our language and interactions that reveal where we are on the burnout spectrum? Are there other communication behaviors we can implement to help guide us away from burnout? The answer is a resounding yes! Let's consider how we approach that yes.

WORKAHOLISM: THE ACCEPTED ADDICTION

As we enter into a conversation about addiction, let me preface by saying that the main goal here is not to cover an exhaustive history of addiction. Rather, our focus is on how healthy callings turn into toxic callings, and ways to readjust and recover when this happens. One way to understand toxic callings is to examine the shift of work as a calling to work as an addiction. If you're reading this and you have personal or family trauma with addiction and want to investigate this further, a few good places to start might be to look into sources like Cloud and Townsend's *Boundaries*, or even Charles Duhigg's *Power of Habit*.

We may feel tempted to rank certain addictions as more problematic than others, couching it much like some do with little white lies. However, before moving too much in that direction, let's review what an addiction really is. Here's what an addiction involves: it starts off as an act that feels good, but slowly it's less about feeling good and more about avoiding the bad feelings from not doing it. Workaholics intentionally and unintentionally tend to twist the truth to serve their need for a fix (e.g., I'll just finish this one work project and then I'll slow down). Employers love workaholics because they are the folks who are always willing to take on more and work longer hours.

Workaholics are usually well-liked because they are reliable in their perceived capacity to take on more and their willingness to say yes, even when others decline. This often results in having more responsibility and social capital. *Social capital* is when we collect positive relationships with others in a way that creates a network of connections and possible opportunities. It's like winning a likability contest.

Workaholism not only impacts our professional lives, it impacts our personal lives as well. Personal relationships and commitments suffer because we view them as secondary. Physical health suffers because we see our bodies as an impediment or obstacle. Have you ever heard someone say, "I wish we didn't have to sleep. I could get so much more done!"? Workaholism means avoiding times of reflection, seeing rest as optional or even evidence of laziness, when really rest and reflection feels incredibly uncomfortable. Why? Because if we keep going, keep moving, keep busy, we don't have to think about things in our lives that aren't working. Productivity becomes the measuring stick of personal self-worth.

Most importantly, when a calling turns into an addiction, the most valuable relationship suffers—our relationship with God. Work becomes a momentary fix rather than a fulfilling expression of who we are. One of the reasons work calling is so prone to move toward workaholism is because of the holy responsibility we feel toward responding to our Caller and making a difference. If we feel called, we see the need and we see how we can help. We sense the Lord moving in us, and it's a wonderful feeling to say "Yes, Lord, use me" and feel him doing just that!

There's a particular kind of intimacy with the Caller when we're actually able to live out our sense of calling. Saying no, even when saying no is the right thing to do, can feel like we are saying no to God and to making something better for others. That bad feeling doesn't actually mean it's bad, and it doesn't necessarily mean we are saying no to God. Setting healthy limits on our work time is a surrendered kind of yes to the Lord, which reminds us who is really in charge and why. It helps us take notice of other parts of our lives that may need attention.

What would it look like to insert these kinds of healthy parameters for those with workaholic tendencies? A common thread among those who manage to stay on the healthy side of calling, rather than allowing it to become a compulsion, includes being able to pause from work for other relational priorities.

For example, Rob, a financial advisor, says this about his bad days, days when his work calling feels unusually hard: "I go home and play with the kids. I am really trying hard these days not to get too caught up in my calling, frankly. You want to be called, but by the same token, you don't want to get sucked in so deeply that it's all you see." Notice, when Rob has bad days at work, he doesn't work *more*. He doesn't set out to prove his worth in work. He takes a break, turns to his family, and remembers what else has value in his life.

If workaholism has taken hold of you, if you find yourself cringing or becoming uncomfortable as you read this section, here's the first thing I want you to know: life doesn't have to keep looking like this. The path from workaholism to burnout is pretty clear. We were literally designed to take a sabbath, being made in the image of God who chose to rest after his work of creating (Genesis 1:26–2:2). When we choose to overwork, letting work attempt to feed our sense of identity in a way only God can, we are choosing to depart from our primary calling—to love God and love others.

Burnout is a liar, and one of its greatest tactics is shame. Here's the second thing: Addictions can't be broken alone. You need others to help you. Needing help is a good thing. Don't put off making a change until tomorrow.

Untangling yourself from this workaholic pace can feel like an uphill process. One good place to start is by apologizing to your family and friends, and then asking a trusted few for help to set new, healthy boundaries. It will be messy, but it's worth it. Freedom tastes so much better than the fake pleasure of addiction.

JOB IDOLIZATION: THE IDENTITY DECEPTION

Recently Allen and I rewatched all of the Indiana Jones movies. Although I'd argue that *Indiana Jones and the Last Crusade* is leaps and bounds better than the rest, it was interesting to note a common thread among them all—the pursuit of an idol. Each adventure is focused on finding an object that promises some danger, but also great wealth, long life, and complete happiness. The characters in the movie dedicate their time, sweat, and even life to finding this object. They sacrifice their morality to grasp hold of a promise of divinity.

What does *idol* actually mean? An idol is generally thought of as an object or person we give our total devotion to and compromise all other things for, in order to literally worship this object or person. From a Christian perspective, it's also more than that.

Idolatry can include offering our complete devotion to anything or anyone other than God. However, it can also look like partial devotion to multiple things or people that collectively seem to offer us complete happiness apart from God (Matthew 6:24; Philippians 3:19). If what occupies our minds, hearts, prioritization, and decision-making process is a driving need for physical security or controllable certainty, a haunting love or desire for material possessions, consuming thoughts of winning approval from others, and intense desires for the outcomes of climbing the social ladder, then the focus shifts from the Caller to us, the called. We know this by another name: pride. If humility is the mother of all virtues, it may be fair to say pride is the generator of all vices.[5]

When our sense of calling becomes more important than the Caller, our calling becomes an idol. When our calling is rooted in our work, and we devote ourselves so much to work that it becomes the thing we revere most, our work calling becomes job idolization.

Although job idolization and workaholism may seem similar due to the way they pull our complete attention away from the Caller, there are distinctions. Job idolization is more about what we see as the *greatest priority* in life. To idolize our work calling means we use work as the decision-making measuring stick under which all other people and goals fall, and the automatic excuse to not show up for other important roles, responsibilities, and relationships that we have. How does this happen? Often very slowly and deceptively, with what may seem like good reasons (my work saves lives, my work will fall apart without me, no one understands and so I must keep going despite the risks and warnings, etc.).

Job idolization happens when work becomes the defining priority (over personal relationships and physical health). To idolize work means to view it as having ultimate importance. Work becomes our god, rather than a place to do good. This toxic calling approach creates a direct path from job idolization to burnout. Replacing the Caller with anyone or anything else means we remove God at the center of our lives, ultimately harming not only our work calling but our general calling, which is to love God and love others. Calling burnout will happen when we lose sight of who God is and who we are.

The reason burnout is more impactful to those who feel called and have succumbed to workaholism and/or job idolization is that it ruptures our core identity. Burnout in general can be detrimental. It can result in deep and consuming feelings of "I don't like what I'm doing anymore." However, remember the difference—burnout from a calling goes beyond that. Burnout from a calling is "I don't know who I am anymore." Questioning our core purpose can feel shameful, disorienting, and devastating.

Are you there right now? Have you become so accustomed to this feeling of burnout that it almost seems normal? Are you attempting to keep it locked up somewhere deep, because it's too hard to admit, or you simply don't have time to be burned out? Perhaps you feel embarrassed that you let it get this far. My friend, burnout may feel definitive, but it does not define you.

BREATH PRAYER AS FRESH AIR

During one of my "almost at burnout" seasons, I came across the practice of incorporating a breath prayer as a way of orienting my spirit toward the Caller. According to Richard J. Foster, breath prayer is based off of the Psalms, where a repeated phrase reminds us of the promises of God or a character attribute of God.[6] It is quite literally a short prayer, often a cry for help, that can be said in one breath.

Foster points to a model example based on the blind beggar sitting by the road, who desperately cried out to the Lord, "Jesus, Son of David, have mercy on me" (Mark 10:47). I set my breath prayer as a reminder that pops up every morning at 11:00 on my phone—late enough into my day that I may have forgotten the impact of my early morning time with God, but early enough to still make a difference. My recent prayer has been: "Let the peace of God rule in my heart" (see Colossians 3:15). So when this Scripture verse pops up, I stop wherever I am and take a breath. As I do, I say this verse. If I can, I speak it out loud.

Why does all of this matter as it relates to calling and burnout? Because a happy consequence of carving out times of reflection like these, even if it is a small moment of resetting, is a reduction of stress, resulting in the ability to deal with stress better and helping us to identify patterns of workaholism or job idolatry sooner. Greg McKeown, author of the best-selling book *Essentialism*, suggests: "We need space to escape in order to discern the essential few from the trivial many. Unfortunately, in our time-starved era we don't get that space by default, only by design."[7] But it almost takes an act of courage to slow down. If we can do this, if we make space to discern our priorities, this makes us better leaders. And when we slow down, it also helps us notice others better. It improves our relationships.

I say this knowing that it's easy to forget. It's easy to forget that in our most stressed-out times, we need to stop and listen for the Caller's voice. Part of the problem is course correction often takes time! If we've been forming unhealthy habits, it takes time to change them. It takes conscious choice to put our lives in positions or places where we can feel the Caller's pleasure.

Before we move on to the next session, would you try something? Remember those three categories resulting from chronic stress (withdrawal, reduced awareness, and tension)? Find a quiet space. Close your eyes and slowly take three deep breaths, in and out. Seriously. Take a moment, and if you're willing, close your eyes. Breathe in and out . . . in and out . . . in and out.

What attribute of God are you most thankful for right now? Thank the Lord for this attribute and tell the Lord what is on your mind and heart at this moment. What are you worried about? Tell him! What are you anxious about? What is causing you stress? Then, consider locating a breath prayer you could say when this kind of stress happens again.

If you're in a season where it's hard to talk to God, perhaps start by using this time to consider what you are most thankful for in your life. Allow a sense of gratitude to wash over you. Then, identify what you're worried or anxious about, the things that are causing you the most stress. Consider finding a phrase that helps you hang on to that gratitude, that helps you remember the good things in your life. Allow yourself to meditate on this for a few moments.

I find that I have to make course corrections all of the time. There's a gravitational pull to compromise our boundaries for the sake of work, of accomplishing, of meeting the needs of others. As a professor, I use the rhythm of the academic calendar to do this. Recently, I realized I was "on the clock" with students at times when I should be focusing on my family or friends (evenings, weekends, etc.). So I decided to create email hours for my students. After talking with three of my mentors about how they budget their time, I formed my own policy. Here's what I said:

> To pursue a healthy professional life, we must also value a healthy personal life. This means learning how to have work boundaries that promote overall wellness. To help model that, Dr. Molloy typically responds to emails Monday–Friday, 8:30 a.m. to 5:30 p.m. Dr. Molloy intentionally chooses Saturday to sabbath, which means she is completely unplugged from all technology. If you email her on Friday after 5:30 p.m., the earliest you will likely hear back from her is Monday morning at 8:30 a.m. If you have not heard back within 48 hours, please feel free to email her again. Reminders are valued.

I talk about it with my students on the first day, encouraging them to develop their own email boundaries. I also put it in the syllabus, online, and repeat it occasionally in class. The hardest part? Sticking to it! If I see an email after 5:30, I am so very tempted to respond to it, simply get it off my plate. I have learned that for me this is a black hole, a deceptive pull to work more than I need to when I don't need to.

What about your own time these days? Is it filled more with anxiety and stress than space to think and reflect on your purpose and calling? There are certainly seasons where you have to push harder than others. But be wary that the season doesn't become your whole life.

Simon Sinek, best-selling author, and well known for a TED talk that remains the third most watched video on TEDtalk.com,[8] suggests that starting with *why*, instead of *how* or *what*, will yield the greatest results.[9] Although this message was designed for the topic of leadership, it is relevant for our conversation as well. If we know the why, we can orient ourselves to all other answers. In the coming chapters, we take time to return to the why of our calling and we turn to what I truly believe is the linchpin of a healthy calling.

The key to remember is that burnout is not selective. It can impact anyone at any time. It is particularly insidious for those who feel called.

GUIDING QUESTIONS

1. Take a moment and consider your own body. It always helps me to close my eyes and breathe in and out. If you're able to do that now, go for it. Eyes closed. Breathing in, breathing out. Then, think about your posture, how you're sitting or standing. Pay attention to your breathing. What do you think your body is saying to you right now?

2. Think back to the three main consequences to sustained stress on our communication: withdrawal, reduced awareness, and physical tension. Which consequence do you recognize most in yourself right now? To help you make sense of this, think through the questions below.

   - Withdrawal: Consider your own circumstances for a moment. Where in your life are you choosing to escape because of stress? Where in your life are you choosing avoidance? It may help to draw a picture or make a list. The goal is to identify where you are seeking escape.

   - Reduced awareness: When you think about your own situation, where in your life have you become overly focused on yourself? Can you think of a time in the past week where, upon reflection, you may have missed cues from other people?

   - Physical tension: Consider your own physical self. How is your body doing right now? When you think about different areas of your life, what would you say is causing you the most exhaustion? How are you physically reacting to situations?

3. Incorporate a breath prayer. What is the cry of your heart right now? Think about your responses to question two.

- Withdrawal: If you're recognizing a pattern of withdrawing, perhaps a breath prayer might be "Father, I draw near to you, please draw near to me" (James 4:8), or "Lord Jesus, give me courage to show up and discernment when I need to say no."

- Reduced awareness: If you've missed moments with people you should have seen or you're feeling overly consumed by your own faults, perhaps your prayer is one about being renewed, asking for eagle-eye vision (Isaiah 40:31). It could be as simple as "I believe, Lord, help me with my unbelief" (Mark 9:24).

- Physical tension: If your body feels war-weary, with internal chaos manifesting itself physically, consider a breath prayer like "Shepherd, please carry me," or "Lord, teach me how to lean on your yoke, to learn your rhythm of grace" (Matthew 11:29).

Consider sharing this breath prayer with a trusted friend, or at the very least place it somewhere you'll see it daily.

ORIENTING PRAYER

Loving God, thank you for your faithfulness. Please forgive me for the areas in my life I have allowed to become an addiction or an idol. I need your help, Lord. I surrender these areas of unhealthiness and ask for your help. Please bring people into my life to help me make healthy changes. Lord, thank you that you are relational. You are not a dictator; you are the Shepherd. You are not an uncaring king; you are the

Wounded Savior. You are not an arbitrary rule-maker; you are the merciful completion of the law as Love. Help me to keep this at the forefront of my mind and heart. Break any hold that shame may have on me, and help me to see you as the loving and relational God that you are. Help me to hear you speak love over me. Amen.

THE LINCHPIN
OF CALLING

THREE

THE THREE Cs IN CALLING'S RELATIONAL CORE

Try this for a moment: Fill in the blank, "Pursuing a calling in my work is important to me because_____."

Now what if you paused here and tried to answer this for a second time? Is there a more "real answer" deeper down, and not the one that's easy to give others or yourself? Or, can you be more specific? Consider closing your eyes and taking a couple of deep breaths. Really think about your sense of calling.

If you're experiencing some of your work as a calling right now, think about the things that ignite a sense of passion and utilize your specific skill sets in ways that feel like the sweet result of hard work and joy mixed together. Or—if you're currently feeling stuck, exhausted, lost, and thirsty for a real sense of living out your calling—think about what you wish you could do if you had the opportunity. And if you don't know how to picture that, if even the idea of meaningful work feels like a grimy window you can't see through, think about the last time you felt a sense of joy in a task or experience of work. What was happening then?

Return to this statement, "Pursuing a calling in my work is important to me because_____." The answer you give here is your *why*. And this why is the orienting factor by which you make sense of all other choices about your work, the compass that directs your future decisions, the plumb line that centers you.

When we are operating in a healthy calling, the answer usually includes some version of the following: *Because when I do it, I feel God's pleasure;*[1] *Because when I'm doing this work it feels like I'm living out what I was meant to do;* or *When I am pursuing my calling, I feel like I am honoring the Lord.* If this does not sound like your answer, if your answer is more like, *Because people need me, Because no one else can do it,* or *Because it makes me feel good in a way nothing else does and I need that feeling to be okay,* something might need to change.

Let's approach it another way. Ask yourself, "Am I currently honoring the Lord by how I am pursuing the calling he has given me? Is anyone suffering because of how I am pursuing it? What can I change about my pursuit of this calling so I am truly loving God and loving others well (including myself)?" If certain answers shed light on what has been in the shadows of your heart, don't reject them. They may cause you to squint internally, but let yourself adjust to this light. This isn't going to be a quick fix. It can be something you learn to pursue and maintain in health. Remember one of the goals—a healthy work calling—should be an expression of who you are, not the definition.

THE COLLECTIVE CONNECTION

One particular summer weekend, my husband, Allen; our young son; and I were staying on Pepperdine University's campus because Allen was the guest speaker for a church retreat. Sadly, the famous Malibu beach views were obscured by curtains of clouds most of the time. However, during one of the retreat breaks, we drove to the Skirball Cultural Center in Los Angeles. If you haven't been there, it's worth the time (and there's an incredible Noah's Ark experiential and exploratory section that will enliven any child for quite some time). Rooted in the rich heritage of Jewish tradition, this venue creates layers of beauty and art, sensorially welcoming visitors. For instance, in the parking lot, in huge, white letters, you'll see "How good and pleasant it is to dwell in community." Taken from Psalm 133:1, this banner welcomes the stranger to join in community, to join in the collective goal of justice, freedom, and equality for all.

In Western cultures, self is the default answer for just about everything. Too often we lead with individualistic thinking, when what's needed is the inclusion of a collective mindset. The same is true in our understanding of calling. One major mistake we make when thinking about calling is the assumption that calling primarily involves the self (my calling, I feel called, etc.). Our callings are not just about us. Some people do consider the role of the Caller as well. This is an important step in the right direction.

Calling is inherently interactive. At the core, at the very center, the basic makeup of our calling is a relational heartbeat. Unlike a hobby, which might be just for ourselves, a calling necessarily involves the one who calls us, so it is an interactive response with the Caller. Yet, there's still a primary element missing. Over the years, as I've interviewed and observed people who operate in their calling, the data reveals something important and often overlooked. There is a third key player: *community*. Calling is pro-social. An essential part of our calling includes those affected by calling and those who influence our ability to actually do our calling.

Therefore, the three "Cs" of calling includes *the Caller* (God), *the called* (you), and *the community* (professional and personal relationships). Understanding this is crucial in knowing how to move forward in a healthy calling. Calling and burnout do not simply impact the self, they impact our relationship with God and our relationships with others.

The interdependent relationships existing in calling point to what calling truly encompasses within the Christian tradition: our sense of calling influences and is influenced by our community.

Consider how the apostle Paul describes the church in 1 Corinthians 12. What metaphor does he use? The body! The body has distinct parts and yet is intricately connected. In this passage Paul admonishes the church to stop thinking so independently, so separately. He reminds us that if we are led by the Spirit of God, we must think and act like members of the same body, which means honoring each part and recognizing how we're all connected, how our roles and actions impact each other.

It's not that we shouldn't think about the personal component of calling, it's more about knowing how the individual and collective are connected. Calling is *integrative* (helps unify), *comprehensive* (impacts every part), and *personal* (experienced differently). How we live out our calling is not a one-size-fits-all, nor is there a hierarchy of "better" or "holier" callings. Recognizing this means learning how to work together, to honor each other's calling as a holy mandate. A healthy relationship with the Caller and with our community is vital in maintaining a healthy calling.

THE FIRST RELATIONSHIP: THE CALLER AND THE CALLED

Regardless of how others may talk about it, calling isn't a tool. It isn't a static, unmoving, unchanging thing. Calling is about dynamic relationships. Like any relationship, our callings may develop or even change over time. Consider the first relational connection in a calling—the Caller and the called. Until we understand that a relationship between the Caller and the called is indeed an ongoing relationship, we either run the risk of trying to be in the driver's seat or we're passively waiting for the car to move. Every healthy relationship involves three things: dialogue (listening and sharing), interaction (doing life together), and maintenance (paying attention when we get off track).

Calling as a back-and-forth process with the Caller does not simply involve a caller; it is defined by interactions *with* the Caller. We read in 1 Thessalonians 5:24, "The one who calls you is faithful, and he will do it." What will God do? He will help us learn the rhythms of a holy life. How will he do it? By teaching us, instructing us, guiding us, interacting with us. Interactions include listening and responding. It means we don't take this relationship for granted. It means we actively protect and care for our relationship with the Caller more than the actual thing we feel called to do.

Living a holy life, a surrendered life, to the Savior does not mean we have to ignore what lights us upside, what gives a deep sense of satisfaction. It means we hold it with an open hand rather than a closed fist. It means we offer our passions and dreams to the Creator, following his direction, trusting he will use us in a known, intimate way, in the way he has designed us. Yes, there will be sacrifice in calling, but sacrifice for what and to whom? For the glory of God, to the Redeemer. Sacrifice to the Savior is always hard and always worth it.

We can look to the way Jesus called his disciples as evidence of this. In passages such as Matthew 4:19, we see how Jesus identified their particular interests and skill sets (fishing). Rather than asking them to ignore or forsake their expertise, he invited the disciples to elevate their giftings, take them to the next level, and learn how to fish for people! Similarly, Luke 5 provides an account of the Caller's miraculous touch to multiply the disciples' catch of fish, in order to help them see what this could mean when they cast their nets for people in the name of the Lord.

We can look at other heroes of the faith and see how they surrendered their fear and trusted God to use their skills and passions for his glory: Moses, who knew what it was to live with royals, served with slaves, protected fearful animals as a shepherd, and guided the people of God as leader. Ruth, who knew what it was to love and lose in marriage, chose courage over fear in family commitments and diverse cultural contexts, humbly listened and trusted the Provider for the care of her mother-in-law and herself. Peter, who knew what it was to risk and succeed or fail, stepped out of the boat and sank, denied the Savior, and returned to his merciful love. Lydia, who knew what it was to succeed in business, attentively listened to the disciples and discerned the truth, taking up the call of financier for Paul's mission.

The same God who called people in history is the God who calls us today. We do not need to fear surrendering to the Caller our longing for a calling. He is the origin of the call, and he is good. When we remember God is good, it changes everything. All else is aligned under this truth: our Caller is good. The one we are in relationship with is good. The danger surfaces when we begin to conflate relationship with him and the actual calling.

Our calling must never be confused with the Caller. Let's repeat that so it really takes root: Our *calling* must never be confused with the *Caller*. We should never place more priority on the gift than the Giver. We might nod to this knowledge, but it's often much harder to keep in order.

It's too easy to start "fitting" God into our schedules rather than orienting our days around time with him. I feel this especially as a parent. Each day seems like a tight matrix puzzle. On the occasion when I have space, my tendency is to want to fill it. A while back, I made a morning agreement with myself: I wouldn't look at my phone at the start of each day until I said hello to God. In his book *The Common Rule: Habits of Purpose in an Age of Distraction*, Justin Earley describes the goal of meeting the Lord in Scripture before meeting the world in our phones.[2]

My morning "hello with the Caller" might be a quick prayer, a moment of silence, a brief reflection on Scripture, or a short devotional (audio devotionals have been a favorite of mine in this season). It doesn't have to be long, but it does need to be intentional. It needs to be the orienting move in a day full of moving pieces. It is a choice to focus on my relationship with the Caller before anything else.

Relationships look different depending on those involved. How do others pursue a relationship with their Caller? Bill, an NFL coach, shared with me, "I think God asks us to take steps and then he directs our path." Similarly, Megan, pastor and chaplain for a police department, explained: "I heard the call through the filter of how can I love God more, how can I respond to him more?" The common thread is relationship, though the experience of relationship may look different.

Relationship involves choice. We choose to lean in and grow closer with the other person or not. For Laurel, painter and art teacher, her work calling rested on the premise that interactions with the Caller are a choice: "When you listen and you heed the call, it's an adventure in faith. Most people will listen; most people don't heed the call." What can we learn from examples such as these? Living out a healthy calling involves mindful and attentive engagement; it prioritizes listening to the Caller and taking action. For people like Bill, Megan, and Laurel, the Caller is not a distant boss; rather, the Caller is a counselor and guide.

What makes for an ideal guide? Guides are most valuable when they are reliable, have accurate knowledge, and maintain some level of communication throughout the journey.

This is good news! We don't have to have it all planned out. We aren't supposed to be the guide! We're supposed to get to know the Guide, follow along with him, and learn from him. This can also feel like bad news for those of us who like a fully developed plan, who want to know what all the steps involve, how long it will take, and what all the risks might be.

I'm an ENFJ on the Myers Briggs and an Enneagram Six. One of the implications of personality tests like this for me is a high value for safety. Also, making lists is part of my love language. In other words, I really like to have a plan. Sometimes I get completely distracted by the pursuit of a plan (e.g., What is it? Am I following it? What's happening next?) and forget the person. When I replace the person with the plan, I get off track. When you think about your own past few weeks, has your focus been on the plan (the calling) or the person (the Caller)?

When trust between the Caller and the called is developed, not knowing the next step doesn't have to feel so overwhelming. Not knowing doesn't have to be a sign of failure. Not knowing is actually part of the process. A calling includes an ongoing attentiveness to what the Caller may be telling us and where he might be leading us. This relational trust is not simply cognitive or emotional trust; it is a complete surrender of the self with the assumption the Caller knows us and cares for us.

Another key step in honoring the relational core of calling is recognizing how our calling impacts, and is impacted by, our community (e.g., how our boss treats us, how our family and friends react to our calling). This is why when we experience calling burnout, it doesn't negatively influence only us; it can harm those we love, work with, and serve alongside. The inverse is also true: those we love, work with, and serve alongside play a mighty role in our experience of calling.

THE FORGOTTEN C

As we focus on the role of community, let's take a minute to define it. While the experience of community may be subjective, some common aspects remain. For our purposes, we understand *community as "an interdependent, socializing space which offers a sense of belonging with an expectation of shared goals and/or values."*[3] That's a bit of a mouthful! Let's break it down step by step.

Consider the first part, *interdependence*. Imagine a continuum, a line with one side being independent (wanting to do everything by yourself) and the other side dependent (completely reliant on others). In communication theory, a healthy relationship is not wholly independent or dependent; rather, it is interdependent. There's a shared trust each person can rely on the other in a mutual give and take, but also each person has their own strengths and abilities to make choices and take action.

A *socializing space* refers to the idea that our professional and personal relationships impact our beliefs about ourselves and the world around us. Our community impacts what we believe is good, possible, and true. In many cases, not only does our community impact our beliefs, they help create and shape them.

Communities also involve an agreed upon value system, or *shared goal*. Communities are formed with a particular goal—to do and/or be something together. Why does this matter in terms of calling? It matters because how we live out our calling is impacted by the support and understanding, or lack thereof, we receive from our community.

Personal communities include our family, friends, book club, flag football team, Pilates partners, church groups, parent groups, or any other gathering whose primary focus is on interpersonal relationships. Professional communities include primary work spaces, volunteer teams, side jobs, or any other group whose primary focus is on accomplishing a task. These groups might function differently. But the way they express care, or lack of care, regarding the value and contributions we make, the way they assign worth to the activities we choose, significantly impacts our long-term ability to pursue them.

Recognizing community as the third C in calling helps us understand the effect of burnout. *Calling burnout cannot be compartmentalized, it doesn't happen only to us; it impacts everyone else in our lives.* Even if we are pursuing a healthy calling, other people in our lives, particularly those who have power over us at work and those who we immediately partner with at home, have the ability to negatively impact our calling and thereby cause toxicity to emerge despite our best efforts.

THE SECOND RELATIONSHIP: THE CALLED AND THE COMMUNITY

In addition to the relationship between the Caller and the called, the other foundational relationship in calling exists within our communities (both professional and personal). With work taking up more than one-third of our adult lives, the connection between community and the underlying meaning of work matters a great deal.[4] And in a time when working from home or remotely is on the rise and work hours bleed into personal life (and vice versa), this is especially pertinent.[5]

With that in mind, what happens when our community (either professional or personal) is at odds with our sense of calling? How much impact does community really have?

Two weeks after graduating college, I was sitting on the back patio of my parents' home. One of their friends was visiting, and over tea and snacks she asked me what I was going to do next. You know, that question of "When are you going to get a real job?" I was familiar with that question from all of the graduation parties and end of the semester gatherings. I had rehearsed answers, but my heart was feeling tender in that moment, so I admitted that I had a part-time job at a church and I was volunteering at a few other places, but I wasn't quite sure what I wanted to do. This friend—who might have been related to Eeyore from the

Hundred Acre Woods, where Winnie the Pooh spent most of his time looking for honey—told me I needed to grow up and just get a job. She adamantly insisted that I didn't need to love it or even like it, I just needed to get a job.

My heart sank because I was aware of my thirst for something meaningful, but I was also quite worried about feeling like a legitimate adult, demonstrating the value of contributing to what seemed responsible. My mother squeezed my hand under the table, and shifted the conversation entirely.

After their Eeyore friend left, my mother looked at me and said, "There may be times in life where you just need to get a job to pay the bills. That's a valid place to be. But you're not there right now. You have the privilege of taking time to figure out what you want to do, to explore what you're good at and what you love. Have the courage to do that! Don't let anyone make you feel bad about this journey."

My friend, do you hear that? Don't let anyone make you feel bad about this journey, your journey. You may be in a situation where paying the bills is the highest priority right now. I've been there. But if you have a desire to pursue meaningful work, don't forsake the longings you have. I truly believe God wastes nothing. In Matthew 11:29, we're invited to learn from Jesus, to learn his ways of doing hard things. He is our teacher, our personal Rabbi, the one who desires to mentor us and show us how to live like Christ. He cares about the details of our lives, and we have the opportunity to proactively learn from him in every circumstance.

Studies have been done on the impact of college students getting asked the question, "When are you going to get a real job?" What they've found is that this question devalues the process that leads up to a full-time work experience.[6] It makes it seem like any preparatory or part-time work isn't real. It's not that the question isn't valid, it's that the judgment within the question serves to reinforce the belief that preparation is separate from outcome. What a sad and disconnected way to view work. When we view work as fitting only one kind of socially acceptable mold, we miss multiple opportunities to learn and grow.

In that first post-college year, I think I may have cried once a week as I swam through uncertain waters, trying to figure out the next "right" move. I would walk my parents' neighborhood block, and just cry.

One rainy Seattle afternoon, my dad saw me wrestling and took me out for coffee. He brought what our family calls his famous pad of yellow-lined paper and a pen. As we sipped our white chocolate mochas, he looked at me with his kind hazel eyes, and said, "Tell me everything you're feeling stressed about." And one-by-one he wrote it down. When I finished sharing, he said, "What else?" I'd dig deep and discover more worries. I'd share them, and he'd write them down.

The incredible Brené Brown, who studies shame and vulnerability, once said something like, "Shame remains the strongest when unspoken." There is something powerful (although scary) about sharing what's plaguing our hearts and minds. Yet, with the right person, the shame deflates and loses its power. So one-by-one my dad and I talked about each weight of worry. When I saw it all on paper, I realized the list wasn't actually as long as it felt cramped up in my own head.

After that, I did three specific things in my post-undergraduate year that really helped: First, I set up short weekly meetings with my parents, with the sole purpose of sharing what I'd learned in my experiences that week and what my goals were for the next week. Outside of those weekly meetings, we agreed that we'd only talk about what I'm doing if I brought it up.

Second, I gave myself a reading list, initially to help me have something to talk about with others during that year of massive uncertainty, where I found myself feeling like I didn't really know what to say. Now, as a professor, this list is one I suggest to my graduating college seniors. I tell them, "Never stop learning! Always have three books you're reading: one book to nourish your spiritual life, one book contributing to your professional goals, and one book that feels like play, that's fun." Because work calling is a dynamic process (it changes over time), a great detriment to pursuing a healthy calling is when we stop intentionally learning. When we do that, our calling can become stale and too often we start to believe we control it, rather than living a surrendered life to our Caller.

Third, during that first post-college year, I also started seeking out coffee times with people I admired or felt curious about in some way. I met with at least two people each month to ask them about their work or life journey. I didn't call it networking at the time, but that's really what it was. And each time I learned more about what actually interested me (or what didn't). Some of the people I met with included a pastor, psychologist, small business owner, nonprofit manager, corporate leader, and professor.

Because my parents honored my preparatory time, and because I tried to honor their support by staying very communicative about my process, I was able to discern that full-time church work wasn't for me. I found a great position at a nonprofit, working for two incredible power-house women. And I learned that although the nonprofit sector scratched some of the itch I had in my heart, ultimately I wanted to learn more . . . so I went back to grad school.

My story would have been so different if I'd ignored the longing to do something personally meaningful, or if my parents hadn't supported that season of exploring. When I felt a lack of support from the pastor I worked for at the church or from well-meaning friends, I was able to go home and talk it through with my parents. Taking time to question what I wanted to do, pushing past the fear of not knowing, and resisting the urge to choose something certain just for certainties sake, allowed me to really get to know what I enjoyed doing and why that mattered.

If your professional and personal community are supportive of your calling, if they also intentionally try to help you achieve it, you are empowered to fully embrace it. However, if your professional and/or personal community does not understand, judges it, or even disdains and resents it, pursuing your calling becomes much, much harder.

Research actually shows that of the options of not ever feeling a work calling and feeling a work calling but being unsupported or restricted in pursuing it, the second option is worse.[7] Those who identify with a calling but are unable to pursue it are more depressed and more dissatisfied in life than those who never identified with a calling. What often gets in the way or propels a person to pursue their calling? Community! Our community makes a difference.

Consider Bethany's situation. She felt called to be a salon manager and hairdresser. Coming from what she referred to as "an East Coast, blue-collar family," Bethany was adamant that anyone can pursue their work as a calling if they want it badly enough to pursue it at all costs. She explained, "Within everybody there's something they love, just need to admit it, face it, pursue it. Nobody was gonna make it happen for me. I had to bite the bullet, find a way to make the money to go to school, admit to my parents this was what I wanted to do."

Work calling does not exist in isolation. What Bethany's story tells us is that not having support doesn't mean the calling can't be pursued. It means we have to decide if we want to pursue it despite the judgment we may experience in our communities. Sometimes we are infused with bravery by the support of our community, and sometimes we must choose to lean into the vulnerability of doing something others don't understand; but we know in the depths of our soul this is our calling.

It is important to seek out someone—or better yet a small handful of someones—whose opinion we trust, who listens well, and who offers wisdom and sound counsel. We should not be pursuing our calling through making choices that will hurt others. And if we see only two options (but either option hurts someone dear in our lives), we need to slow down and pray that God shows us a third option. God is the Creator. He is the waymaker. We have seen in the pages of Scripture that his presence divides oceans, crumbles rock walls, multiplies loaves and fish, tears thick curtains, and conquers what feels unconquerable. If we offer our circumstances to him, he is able to make a third option. He is the same God we know today. We must be careful not to let impatience make it seem like urgency is more important than doing the right thing.

When you think about your own community, who comes to mind? Are they people in your workplace, personal relationships, or both? There may be only one or two—it doesn't have to be a large group to make a community. The point is not how big your community is, but who you go to for counsel, for help, to share everyday concerns and hopes.

With work taking up so much of our adult lives, it's not uncommon to find our greatest sense of community at work. Having a healthy work community can feel amazing. However, it can also get complicated when we confuse workplace relationships with family relationships, especially when there is actual overlap.

PROFESSIONAL COMMUNITIES

Broadly speaking, as we're talking about professional community, let's think of it as any kind of relationship you might have with those who are a part of your work world. These relationships could be manager-employee, peer-related, or partnering groups. The feeling of community might exist most within a specific department or team, or among the organization as a whole. *Professional communities* refers to the interpersonal interactions you have with those you work for, with, and who work for you. They are the people with whom you must learn to navigate conflict, decision-making outcomes, and the collaboration processes all for the primary purpose of task-related goals.

Some work communities are very informal, not just in the "casual Friday" sense, but in how they speak with each other, what they speak about, the kind of work schedule and location expected, and their general levels of transparency. For example, in some work groups you might pray together at the start, share personal stories about family celebrations and crises, or even feel free to cry in front of each other. In other work communities, you might be expected to create as much of a compartmentalized life as possible, where personal life "stays at home" and professional life means doing what's expected of you in a timely manner. In many situations it's somewhere in the middle.

Healthy work communities might honor a culture of calling collectively, or find that their specific work responsibilities naturally help them embrace calling. In some cases, the desire to be part of a culture of calling can even sway people to move to different companies. Carrie, a nonprofit financial development officer, reflected on her recent work transition, noting how her new colleagues talked about their work during an orientation meeting: "They all used this sense of calling in describing their work. I feel like from talking to the other people in the organization that everybody is there because they have this sense of calling." Carrie's workplace provided a relational bond from shared beliefs and resources.

When I speak with college students who are considering post-graduate work, they often ask me what kind of work to pursue. I share that sometimes being part of a work culture that collectively values a sense of calling is more meaningful than the actual tasks they might personally get assigned. Other times, the particular work role might make more of a difference to them, what they are allowed to pursue and master.

For Grant, vice president at a digital advertising agency, it was less about an overall organizational culture of calling and more about how his specific role in the company allowed him to embrace his calling: "What draws me more is being the guy for the company that ensures our clients are taken care of, make sure our employees come first. What I like to do, I think ultimately, is invest in people." The constant thread here is the prosocial nature of calling. Knowing our work makes a positive difference in the lives of others is key.

What can we learn from examples such as these? First, calling is about relationship. Second, workplaces where a culture of calling is explicitly encouraged can literally inspire people to want to work there. This can be done through an overall sense of organizational culture or through helping people identify ways in which their roles allow them to pursue this approach. Third, the quality of relationships within professional contexts has a direct impact on our experience of a work calling. When we are able to live out our work calling among those who understand this approach and even seek to encourage it, work can feel enlivening.

Perhaps one of the most poignant examples in my own research of the way our calling impacts our community and our community impacts our calling, was when I interviewed Josh, an acupuncturist specializing in infertility treatment. Located in the heart of the city in a large, old building with several other businesses, I remember meeting him in his office for the first time. I immediately noted two of the four walls in his office were almost entirely covered with baby pictures, family pictures, and thank-you cards from his clients. The visual impact of these two walls provided a frame of interaction with community, a marker of solidarity and commemoration.

Throughout our interview, a few women would come in and sit in the waiting area. We'd stop the interview each time, while he took them to an inner room for acupuncture treatment. One woman pulled out a picture of her latest ultrasound and showed Josh, saying in a kind of whisper cry, "What am I going to bring to Josh today? Because everything I bring, you fix." Josh's impact on his patients was not only represented in his interactions with them, it was obvious in the actual space of his walls, through the pictures: successful conception and restored dreams.

Whenever we had to stop our interview for him to welcome a patient, I'd stand up and look over the hundreds of baby and family pictures. Thank-you cards, which were also posted all over the wall, included phrases like, "When all the other doctors told us there was no hope, we came to you. A month later, we were pregnant."

Toward the end of the interview, Josh talked about being successful in his work calling. I asked, "What does success look like for you?"

Josh gestured with his hands toward the walls, "I mean these pictures are a constant reminder of the positive changes that I've helped people make in their lives, and it's just a very comforting wall for me." Josh's walls represent the work he feels called to do and the necessary interaction involved with the community of patients and their families.

There is a dark side, however. When organizations as a whole, or people in power within a workplace, appeal to the relational quality of a person's calling in order to get them to work more hours, take on more responsibilities, and ignore personal boundaries, our callings are in danger of becoming toxic. Two ways this can happen are when we confuse work with family and when we stop listening to real concerns.

Work is not your family. People tend to like the metaphor of family when describing a work climate because it captures the sense of belonging, purposeful connection, shared experiences, and deeply held values or goals.[8] Here's the problem: we don't fire family. We do fire employees. Here's another problem: in a family, there are parents/adults and there are kids. This gives license for parents to make decisions or treat their kids in a certain way that would not be appropriate for the workplace. Depending on the age of the child, a parent may expect full obedience with no questions asked. There are rules for a child that are not the same as for the parent or adult.

To apply the metaphor of a parent/child relationship within the family is not an appropriate expectation of a boss or manager. This does not honor the adulthood, let alone skill set and experiences, of their employees. In Christian organizations and ministries, we might all relationally be "brothers and sisters in Christ," but occupationally we should be careful when extending this family metaphor.

Within family-owned businesses this can get especially complex, and there are some unique expectations and ways of doing things in a family-owned business that may not apply for other workplace contexts. However, generally speaking, family means forever; work relationships do not. In work, we can be a team, we can be a community, we can be a village. In those instances, people leave or are told to leave, and it's not necessarily a betrayal.

How does a calling move from what can be a powerfully compelling and positive way of living, to a toxic and harmful work approach? It often starts with a slow shift, a slow creep of unwise everyday work practices. So what can be done? Paying attention to ways we talk about our work, as well as how other people communicate with us at work and about work, is the starting place. Paying attention to communication is like using a stethoscope to listen to your heart, or an x-ray to look at your bones. It reveals quite a lot.

Let's start with how others talk with us at and about work. Remember, community suggests an ongoing dialogue, with an expectation of continued exchange of ideas and common values. In healthy professional communities, power and decision-making are shared, at least to some degree.

One sign of an unhealthy community is found in the use of *discursive closure*.[9] This is when someone uses language to shut down the conversation, resulting in the feeling of being unable to voice a difference of opinion, ask further questions, or seek alternatives.

Here are some prime examples of discursive closure: Someone might say, "It's not personal, it's business." One worker shared with me that they tried to speak with their boss about feeling overworked, and the boss replied, "We're all feeling overworked. It's a calling, so we make sacrifices." In both instances, the person in power closed down the conversation through discourse. For example, the use of the word *sacrifice* has a holy connotation to it. But make no mistake, a sacrifice is the willingness to give something (or someone) up with the expectation of no return. It must be voluntary. A more appropriate word to use might be *responsibility*, because that's a fair workplace value. However, the word *sacrifice*—the appeal to something holy—can make the worker who is called feel as if they have no choice but to submit.

In one instance, a friend came to me to ask for advice. They were getting bullied at work, at a Christian workplace, and the response from their boss was, "There's really nothing I can do. It's not quite an HR case. You just really need to pray about it." Using spiritual language to close down a conversation is wrong. Additionally, this response actually diminishes what prayer is and doesn't address active watchfulness, that helpful partner to prayer. If you find yourself in a position of leadership and someone comes to you with a concern or complaint, be careful of using responses to silence that person.

Now, discursive closure isn't always intentional. Often, it's an unthinking or exhausted response. It comes from not really listening. But *impact*, how it makes someone feel, and *intent*, what was actually meant, are not the same.

Healthy communicators make time for questions like, "Did I take a moment to try and understand where this person is coming from?" Healthy communicators stay curious and assume there's more they might need to know: "What else should I learn about this person or situation before moving on?" Healthy communicators honor what the worker feels is sacred and seek to help them apply it for the right reasons. They do not use emotional, relational, spiritual appeals to get workers to do more with less (less pay, less acknowledgment, less resources). Using a person's calling to influence them to ignore their own boundaries is harmful, lazy, and selfish. We must do better. We must be better. In this way, we hold some responsibility to help others steward their calling.

Helping each other stay accountable in the pursuit of healthy calling means honoring boundaries. Work boundaries are essential in a healthy calling, not just in consideration for ourselves but in the way we honor others. When we help others learn how to apply work boundaries well, we stay mindful that work is not the ultimate source of identity definition (job idolatry). Work boundaries also help us remember how to feel good outside of work, instead of being addicted to it (workaholism).

The tricky part is that work boundaries are a process and they are subjective. They require maintenance, flexibility, and (re)clarification. People also have different work capacities. This means learning about your own capacity—how much is too much—and learning about others' capacities. Certainly, when economic downturns or organizational changes occur, it may be necessary for everyone to pitch in and do more for a while. The key is to stay mindful of how long this is needed and how each person can bend and flex. If this happens, be sure there is an agreed upon time to end the intensity, or to revisit whether it is still necessary and how that might impact other aspects of those involved. This might need to happen several times when contexts remain uncertain.

PERSONAL COMMUNITIES

Not only is work calling connected to professional community, it is significantly impacted by and impacts personal community.

It's the small things. It's the little comments, the almost unseen actions, that build into a strong memory. Memories are formative, taking root and adding shape to who we are. Notable civil rights activist Marian Wright Edelman says it this way: "We must not, in trying to think about how we can make a big difference, ignore the small daily differences we can make which, over time, add up to big differences that we often cannot foresee."[10] Although the workplace may serve as a great site of interaction in adulthood, it is through daily personal, and especially familial, communication where much of our initial understanding of the world is formed.[11] In fact, the influence of communication within the family makes a long-lasting impact upon our personal and professional development.

Memorable messages are those firmly rooted in communication and, known for being memories formed during childhood or adolescence, they remain at the forefront of our mind and have made significant influence on our life. If I were to ask you to reflect on the most memorable message you can remember receiving from a parent (or guardian) regarding work or the meaning of work, what would come to your mind?

I have a very strong memory of being seven years old, sitting at the dinner table while my parents talked about their work. They were making a shift from pastoral ministry to real estate, and the transition made finances tight for a while. They freely spoke about their work at the table on a regular basis, inviting me into the conversation and even talking about what I did at school as work. Typically, we'd each answer the question "How was your day?" in great detail. And we'd really listen as we shared our responses.

This particular time, I got up from my chair and returned with my piggy bank full of coins. I emptied it on the table and said I wanted to contribute to what our family needed. My dad tried to give me back the coins, but I was adamant. He told me we can trust in God as our Provider—"Whatever money we have is his anyway," he said with steady eyes. Both of my parents worked several jobs for a while during this transition and in this season; they also had weekly designated "date" times with me. I felt the strain but I didn't feel less loved. My dad still has those same coins in a bag on his desk today.

This memory formed in my mind a message about work impacting family and family impacting work: that we all share in the process together, and faith and action make great partners. Now as an adult, my husband and I talk about our days, including our work, with our son at the dinner table. We talk about his time at school as work, too. We listen, learn, and support each other.

Memorable messages can act as personal proverbs individuals use to interpret their world. So let's turn to the role of community for a moment. What is a memorable message about work you received from your personal community? How does that impact you today?

In my own research, some participants commented on difficult family situations as direct influences on their work calling. Katie, a palliative care social worker, points to being "instilled" with a work calling because of learning how to take care of her chronically ill father. Parents were not only credited for cultivating a work calling in their children, they were also referenced as models for what kind of work approach to avoid.

When asking Stephen, a wealth manager, who or what influenced his work approach, he explained: "I grew up with a dad that was never home. When he was at home, he was locked in his den doing all the administration on his business. I never had interaction with Dad. It created a value in my system to make sure when I'm home, I'm home with my wife and my kids. We're together as a family. I don't do any work on the weekend." Here, a core value of an appropriate work calling developed from intentionally choosing to stop a particular cycle of parenting. Stephen chose not to continue the behavior of a distant, overworked dad. Instead, the health of Stephen's work calling is predicated on the health of his family life.

The dark side of personal community and the impact of their communication around calling can be seen in feeling what's called *job judgment*. Sort of like adult peer pressure, job judgment is when others label your work as not real or not of value. Interestingly, among general society if you like your work in a way that's seen as too much, if it's seasonal, temporary, or unpaid work, or if it's not the primary means of financial support or has a low probability of success, it is viewed as "not real."[12] Who does this approach to work leave out? Groups such as volunteers, interns, many who are self-employed, those who work from home, parents, artists, many nonprofits, and even professional athletes.

Other people's views on our work are hard to ignore, or at the very least hard not to give power to in guiding our choices. Part of pursuing a work calling is being able to withstand job judgment. One way to withstand job judgment is to keep your calling priorities straight. Stay focused on your relationship with the Caller. Stay mindful of the actual communities you get to impact. Rather than fighting so hard to be understood by everyone, which is a very normal need, shift the goal. What do you know to be true and what do you value? Who helps you remember this? Make interactions with them a priority.

Another complexity of personal community and calling, especially among family, is intergenerational calling pressures.[13] For example, first generation immigrant parents might feel like it's their calling to work hard enough so their children have a better life. This is often identified by the children attending prestigious colleges, graduating with a contract for a well-paying job in hand, and helping ensure security for the family. At the same time, the second-generation adult children may feel the pressure of their parents' calling as they seek to locate their own understanding of meaningful work.

Although it can be complex, there is a bright side of personal community's communication about calling. It can be the birthplace for inspiration and belonging. For example, Mark, a publisher and entrepreneur, shared, "In many ways I followed in my dad's footsteps to not go down the corporate track, to create my own future and the confidence that I can go out and do it." Parents have the potential to be the greatest teachers about meaningful work. As Nicole, a massage therapist, explains, "My work ethic, from my roots, would be my father. He always told me from an early age: It doesn't matter how much money you make, enjoy what you're doing."

Parents play a vital role in the way their children think about (and pursue) work. If you are a parent or thinking about becoming a parent, stay mindful that you get to help shape the worldview of your children as it relates to work calling. During one interview with Frank, a primary care doctor, I noticed his grandchildren's drawings and pictures of his daughter and two grandsons in every room of his practice. Frank saw me noticing them, leaned forward, and shared: "Everybody says they have cute grandkids. You know the best part? This is how they are inside. That's my secret. People go, 'Oh, my grandkid is smart.' Oh, these kids are very smart. And 'My grandkid is beautiful.' But my grandkids are beautiful on the inside. And why? Because of that girl right there." Frank points to the photo of his daughter. "Their mom." His pictures revealed the value he placed on his family, the legacy of his parenting, and the inclusion of his grandkids as a sign of his success.

Frank continued to make direct connections between success in his personal community with his work calling. He pointed to the success of his family as indicative of a healthy work calling enactment, sharing, "My father's life didn't work out the way he would have liked. He wound up working in a little grocery store with his aging father. He never wanted that life for me." Frank continually spoke of the sacrifices his own father made to ensure that he would not have to be limited in his work options. His dad laid the framework for Frank's work calling. Whether it is teaching by example (of what to do or not to do) or by direct conversations, interactions with parents significantly influence our understanding of work as a calling.

COMMUNITY IMPACT AND BURNOUT

Why does it matter that a calling involves three distinct players? It matters because as we take time to uncover the layers of burnout, we need to understand how it impacts our relationships, with our Caller, with our communities, and even with ourselves. It matters because when we consider what it takes to protect our calling, to avoid and recover from burnout, we need to recognize the way we communicate about our calling must come from a place of humility.

Work calling is not a compartmentalized function of work; it is a way of being. We cannot have a healthy work calling if it hurts our personal community. For example, Bill, the NFL coach, acknowledged that his work calling significantly impacted his family life, and his family life necessarily impacted his work calling. He shared how his work requires him to be away from home during a large portion of the year, prioritizing his team. To combat this, he and his wife designate a special dinner after each football season is over to talk about how things are going. "Because," as he shared, "I didn't want her to just survive, I wanted her to thrive."

Bill paused for an extended time, then asked: "You ever seen the movie *The Little Mermaid*? There's this mean octopus lady named Ursula. When she casts those spells on those merpeople, did you see those little oyster shells all shriveled up? I try to make sure my family doesn't look like that."

Bill's story underscores a tension in the pursuit of managing the priorities of work as a calling and of family. If his work calling starts demanding the sacrifice of his family, it is no longer a virtuous calling. Work calling can cause our family relationships to implode, to wither and lose any form of identity. Unless we remain vigilant of the dark side to work calling, we run the risk of a toxic calling.[14]

The worries of this life have a funny way of choking out our joy. Jesus talks about this in the parable about the sower of the seeds. In Matthew 13:7, he specifies that some of the seeds (people) fall among the thorns, which he says are the worries of this world. We are impacted by the people and circumstances in our lives. Our calling is impacted by the kind of environment we surround ourselves in. And because a calling is about living out our passion and skills in work, it has the potential to push work beyond the healthy boundaries of a well-balanced life.

If your professional and/or personal community is negatively impacting your experience of calling, what can you change? What do you currently have control over? Can you change who you interact with on a routine basis? What if you limit interactions that suck the air out of your lungs? Or you regularly seek out someone who reminds you of what is good and possible?

I was part of a text thread with a group of people I really admired, but the space for safely venting became too heavy for me. Although I enjoyed the people, I realized I needed to stop reading the texts. My heart and mental state were too impacted by the messages exchanged. On the flip side, one of my best friends and I set up a once-a-week, one hour check-in time (either by phone or in person). She and I help each other see the light when things feel dark, in whatever kind of messy way we may be feeling. She is safe and I feel seen with her.

Is there a task you can alter that might bring you greater joy or meaning in the relationships it involves? Or are you able to delegate certain tasks so you can reduce interactions with those who negatively influence your sense of calling?

As a professor, meeting with students brings me joy. I also carry what they are dealing with in my own heart long after meeting. I learned I needed to pace out, and space out, how many students I met with each week so I can have a fresh heart and mind for them, for myself, and for my family. Sometimes if my office hours are full, but a student wants to meet, I have to weigh the cost. Is it time-sensitive or an emergency? If it is, we find a way to meet. If not, and I've reached my capacity, I need to keep my office-hour structures intact and point them to another resource for the time being.

Remember, calling is a relationship between the Caller and the called. When you are weary with the weight of the world, turn to that relationship to be refreshed. Draw near to your Caller and he will draw near to you! Jesus invites us to come to him. He assures us that he will give us rest. Offer him your full plate, your burdens. He's a good creator; he's the master artist. He's the best organizer. He will help you tend your seeds well.

Imagine for a moment if you really believed this about your work: God cares for you, he knows your fears, and he is fully aware of your unspoken dreams. He wants to help you.

GUIDING QUESTIONS

1. Who we choose to listen to plays a significant role in our pursuit and experience of work as a calling. Who are you talking to these days about your calling?

   - Are they listening to you? Do you feel supported?

   - How does this impact your pursuit of calling now?

   - We aren't meant to do this alone. Who could you reach out to if you need more support right now?

   - If you don't have anyone in your life, look beyond the people you know and pursue authors you admire, podcasters you follow, bloggers or vloggers who seem to "get it." Let them reach out to you through pages and speakers, to help support you.

2. Think back to ways we might shift our morning routines so it feels more honoring to the Caller (e.g., no phone until greeting the Lord). What's something you could try this week to help frame your day with a mindset of prioritizing your relationship with the Caller?

- Rather than make a big goal, consider a small, achievable step.
- After one week, assess whether this works for you or not. It may take a few tries. Remember, it isn't about what you can perfect that makes it work, it's about how this process directs your focus.

3. Return to your memorable message about work you received from someone early on in your life: What part of that message do you want to keep now?

- Is there any part that you'd want to change?
- If the answer is yes, how would you change it? If the answer is no, how can you be more intentional of keeping this memory fresh as you pursue your calling now?

4. Think about your current relationships. On a scale of one to five (five being "my personal community is doing really well" and one being "the people in my personal community are barely hanging on"), how would you rate the health of your professional and personal communities?

- How do you think the people in your community might respond to these questions?

ORIENTING PRAYER

Lord, I believe you are able to make a way where there appears to be no way. I know you can create pathways I cannot see. You are the divider of seas when I need to cross oceans. Help me to trust you with my calling. Help me to prioritize you as my Caller. Please forgive me for times where I may have confused the two. Please show me how to have a healthy work calling; please direct me toward healthy work practices and people. Please help me to be mindful of the messages I give and receive about work, both in my professional and personal communities. More than anything, help me to glorify you in my approach to work. My dearest Lord, my faithful Caller. Amen.

FOUR

THE MISUNDERSTOOD
AND UNDERREPRESENTED
ROLE OF HUMILITY

One of my favorite college courses to teach is Communication and Calling.[1] On the first day I ask my students, "If someone took care of your finances for one year, so it wasn't something you had to worry about, and you could have any internship or starting job you wanted, what would it be? What would your dream internship look like?" I ask this for several reasons: I want them to dream and think past the initial fears and doubts. I want them to uncover what really motivates and energizes them.

If asked the same question, what would your answer be? Imagine if all of your bills and life demands were taken care of for one year. What would uninterrupted time of fully immersing yourself in some kind of work you care deeply about actually look like? Now, consider how closely aligned your answer is with what you're presently pursuing.

For me, it would be what I am currently doing . . . mostly. Perhaps with fewer committee meetings and less grading, and a few more late-start mornings, allowing for cooking, reading for fun, and a run by the beach. But teaching and mentoring students, researching, writing, and speaking about important topics like calling and burnout—this really is my work calling! It is what I *want* to be doing.

I know experiencing work as a calling is a gift and a privilege. I don't take it lightly. A large portion of my life I felt vocationally lost, ashamed of living in such uncertainty, and marked as a non-legitimate adult. That last year of college and the cluster of years post-college were entirely disorienting for me as I tried to figure out what I should be doing, what I wanted to be doing, and what I could do. I see similar struggle with people in midlife (forties and fifties) as well as those facing or currently in retirement (late sixties and early seventies). There are key times in life when we find ourselves in a new season of uncertainty, and it is in those seasons we are either refined or reduced in our sense of what is possible and what is good.

Maybe you've had this experience at some point. Maybe you're living it right now. Feeling lost in what to do, what to pursue, what value you might bring, where you can offer your skills and passions, or even what those skills and passions might be at this point. As you try to figure this out, do not for one moment give in to the temptation that you have nothing to offer. Do not for one moment think your time is over or the best has already passed you by. Our God is the Creator, and he is ever-creating. You matter. What you have to offer matters. You might feel messy right now, but messy isn't bad; messy is part of the process in producing something beautiful. You might feel used up and dried up. If that's you right now, know that as I'm writing this, I pause and I am praying for you. Right now, I am asking God to cover you with his care.

It is truly hard to keep hope alive sometimes. But here's the deal: it isn't your job to keep hope alive. God's holy Word reminds us our anchoring hope is Jesus (Hebrews 6:19). He is our hope. Our job is to tether ourselves to him.

As a college student, I transferred from one college to another and changed my major multiple times. Sitting in classes, discussing topics of varying interest, I never quite felt at home. I remember laying on the floor of my parent's living room, wrestling with what major to choose, saying, "I know how to be a daughter—is that a profession?" I really didn't know what I wanted to do, or even what that want would feel and look like.

I remember seeing the same angst with some of my friends who actually did know what they wanted to do in college, but the angst came later for them. As they reached their late twenties, they realized the kind of work they initially chose no longer met their internal needs. It no longer felt purposeful. The search for purposeful work became a journey. And because calling is a dynamic process, it is still a journey.

To be clear, I don't feel a strong sense of calling *all* the time. There are hard days and monotonous days. But about 80 percent of the time, I'd choose my current work over any other, no question. As Erin, a school psychologist, confided, "I feel personally called to my work, and there are still a lot of days where if someone said, 'Do you want to go home right now?' I'd say, 'Yeah.' So don't confuse having a slow day with not being called to something." Calling is both a thrilling experience and a commitment despite current feelings.

In fact, in my interviews with people, they referred to *calling* in metaphors of both falling and being in love. For example, as two people are falling in love, there are high highs of joy and everything seems a little bit rosy, whereas couples committed to being in love will experience moments of deep joy as well as moments of real hardship.

Years ago, my parents taught marriage classes. I remember them coming home and talking about what they shared with newly engaged couples. They described committed love as a cycle: *romance* (the initial stage where everything's amazing and almost magical); *reality* (the moment when you say, "Oh my goodness, I can't believe I didn't notice this super annoying, frustrating thing about this person . . . I don't know if I want to be in this"); and *joy* (when it's the right relationship, making the decision to choose that person, for good and bad seasons, in times of hardship. Falling forward instead of pulling back in pursuit of health, recognizing the need for boundaries and ongoing care).

Sticking with this decision moves the *joy* back to *romance* and then *reality*, and so on. Calling is both a kind of falling in love (moments of deep elation) and being in love (commitment and investment in relational maintenance).

GOING THROUGH THE TUNNEL

As we recognize the value and merit of calling, as well as the dark sides, we must understand there will be wonderful times and there will be hard times. In the case of pursuing and experiencing work as a calling, there will be moments when we feel totally and fully alive in our sense of doing what we were meant to do. There may also be moments when we've gotten entangled in the hard parts and feel dangerously close to burnout or, even worse, dangerously consumed by burnout.

There are certainly decisions we can make to help us avoid burnout (e.g., not getting sucked into workaholism or job idolization), but even with the best of intentions, burnout may still occur. And when it does, we can't go over it. We can't go under it. We can't go around it. We must go through it. We must go through the tunnel of burnout to get to the other side.[2] How can this be done without being completely overcome, without getting entirely stuck?

As we explore our callings more deeply, we come to recognize both the bright and dark sides of calling and, more specifically, the dangers of calling burnout. Approaching burnout with discernment means recognizing the slippery slopes toward workaholism or job idolization. Discernment in our calling also means identifying how our communities, in both professional and personal relationships, can constrain or empower our lived experiences of calling.

This is not the pessimist's nor the optimist's road. This is wisdom's road. And wisdom begins with humility. In fact, I'd like to suggest that humility is the linchpin. Humility is what helps us manage burnout and pursue our callings in sustainable, healthy ways. Humility helps us avoid some of the burnout tunnels that lay ahead. And humility is the best process by which we are able to get through the tunnels of burnout and reach the other side.

For many of us, humility can have negative or simply uninteresting connotations. It's easy to think of is as synonymous with being passive, or coming across as lacking confidence. But that is not the case. In this chapter, we bring light into the muddy shadows of humility myths, by addressing the main ways people incorrectly approach humility, the value of understanding humility as a specifically relational virtue, and the key role gratitude plays in walking humbly with God as our Caller.

DEBUNKING OUR APPROACH TO HUMILITY

Some of the best things in life are ones we didn't plan for—and I certainly didn't mean to get involved in the topic of humility. Two years into my full-time job as a professor, I was growing more and more curious about the dark side of calling, and in my third year (as I mentioned in the Introduction) I had my first *major* adult burnout crisis. There had been previous burnout moments, like in my doctorate program. But this was different.

This particular time of burnout wasn't simply because I was in a seasonally intense time (e.g., graduate school, getting married, being the parent of a toddler, caring for a sick loved one, or starting a new business). This was my everyday life, and I was burned out with no hope of change unless I initiated it.

In my fourth year as a professor, I received a research fellowship that was part of a larger program called The Center for Christian Thought, which gave space for scholars to consider Christian virtues as it related to their discipline. This particular fellowship focused on humility, and allowed me time to basically binge-watch research for a semester.

Over the course of sixteen weeks, the other scholarly fellows and I met in a cozy room with dark cherrywood furniture on campus, eating really good food and sharing ideas and research on humility. I'll be totally honest, I applied for this opportunity both because I was intrigued by the study of humility, and also because it offered two course releases, which meant my teaching load would be cut back quite a bit. I could feel myself starting to break down and this fellowship offered a welcome change to slow the pace.

What I didn't realize is how much I would enjoy being in a primary learning role again. It felt like I was part of the Inklings, the group where great scholars like C. S. Lewis and J. R. R. Tolkien would gather to sharpen their skills. Drinking from the firehose of dense literature and soaking in complex conversations, although challenging, was so refreshing. My mind and heart would start sparking when I sat down to study the next expert researcher on humility. And it didn't take long for me to realize there was a very clear connection between what I was studying (calling and burnout) and humility. It was like a picture slowly coming into focus.

In that season of communing with other scholars, I began to realize that humility is approached very differently by different people. Have you had that experience, when you thought something was universally understood, but in reality people approach it with varied interpretations? Maybe you and those you live with think differently about what is restful or what a clean house looks like. Perhaps you're constantly amazed that people have different perceptions about what it means to be a good driver.

During this research fellowship, I learned that humility is not a universally understood term. Even expert scholars have diverse interpretations of what humility looks like.[3] And this is highly significant.

For our purposes, it's vital that we locate a common understanding of humility. What's especially important is that if we identify as a Christian, walking in humility helps us walk with God. In Micah 6:8 we are literally told that humility is something God *requires* of us: "And what does the Lord require of you? To act justly and to love mercy and to walk humbly with your God." Humility is something we should actively pursue because it is the makeup of the wise.

Let's slow down for a moment here, so we can really take this in: humility is an indication of wisdom. It has absolutely nothing to do with being ignorant, foolish, or unaware. Rather, humility is how we are to enter into the process of walking with God, which means properly understanding humility is essential. For when we humbly walk with God, our eyes are fixed on him. Our calling is oriented by the Caller.

THE BIG MYTH ABOUT HUMILITY

Throughout Scripture, humility is seen as a holy virtue, worthy of pursuit, and something that actually helps us (e.g., 2 Chronicles 7:14, Proverbs 22:4, James 3:13, and Philippians 2:1-11). In fact, God's Word reveals a critical point: if we are to be like Christ, we must not only pursue humility as the key virtue, we must adopt it as a core attribute in apprenticing Jesus. For example, Ephesians 4:2 tells us, "Be completely humble and gentle; be patient, bearing with one another in love." This isn't just an urging to be a little bit humble. It's a charge to be entirely humble. This isn't just a mandate for women, or for men, nor for those in power or those under power. It is for all of us.

Humility is *the* central virtue in which all other virtues arise and without which no other virtue can thrive. Pastor and spiritual writer Andrew Murray goes so far as to say that pride is not simply the loss of humility, but it is actually evil, whereas the humility of Christ is our literal salvation. If being like Christ means being humble, why would we ever think being humble means being unaware or naïve? Christ is neither of those things. Murray echoes this, suggesting humility is one of the most misunderstood and unexamined essentials in Christianity and the church. Why?

The problem is that today we tend to confuse humility with a *lack of confidence* (a type of self-imposed ignorance of the skills and passions God himself gave us), a shy *passivity* (never speaking up for ourselves), or even a *dismissal of boundaries* (believing we have to serve and serve and serve, sacrificing rest, until we reach burnout). Just a reminder, burnout is not a badge to proudly wear as a decorative statement of commitment. Burnout is a thief and a liar.

Some of this confusion about humility is rooted in the myth that humility is synonymous with modesty. Humility and modesty often look the same and can overlap, but they are indeed distinct.

An identity of humility is different than an identity of modesty. An identity of modesty may be focused on avoiding attention, even to the point of belittling our accomplishments, whereas an identity of humility, as C. S. Lewis so appropriately said, means "not thinking less of yourself, it's thinking of yourself less."[4] Thinking less of yourself is thinking poorly of yourself. It is being consumed with your own faults and failures, which is really just a different kind of unhealthy focus on the self (also known as pride). On the flip side, if you're thinking of yourself less, it means your focus is on something other than yourself.

The humble person thinks of others, viewing them as those who are made in the image of God. The humble person is not looking to "people please," but to please God. In this way, the humble person is not blind to their own strengths, because they are looking to see how their strengths can help others. They are self-aware without being self-consumed.

Counter this with a person who is typically known as modest. A modest person may not seek attention or wish to be the center of things, but it is not a guarantee they are aware of themselves at all. Jane Foulcher, author of *Reclaiming Humility: Four Studies in the Monastic Tradition*, suggests it is a significant mistake to conflate humility with modesty, tracing the error back to the days of Thomas Aquinas. In Aquinas's effort to connect Christianity with Aristotelian thoughts on the good life, modesty and humility were discussed interchangeably. However, Foulcher argues, they are distinct. What is lost in sheer modesty, even on the best days, is a relational quality necessary in understanding the "radical implications of mutual humility."[5]

A modest person looks down, not seeking attention. A humble person looks out and up, seeking to connect with others.

Let's take it a step further. To communicate with humility is different from communicating with modesty. A modest person may intentionally avoid attention, seeking to cover up or even deny any evidence of strengths, whereas a humble person communicates in confidence but without seeking to prove anything. They may communicate with warmth and friendliness, full of life, but they are not after attention. The humble person is after the care of others.

This is why leadership books like the famous *Good to Great* by Jim Collins or *The Ideal Team Player* by Patrick Lencioni connect humility with other virtues we don't often think to pair it with— healthy ambition, or a good work ethic.[6] Actual, true humility makes for a great leader, a fantastic team player, an excellent friend, a successful romantic partner, and a happy parent.

And it isn't just about leaders being humble. Professor and ministry trailblazer Dennis Edwards, author of *Humility Illuminated,* suggests humility can empower those who feel marginalized with an authentic focus on justice work and multiethnic ministry.[7] When enacted in a biblical framework, Edwards argues, humility is groundbreaking.

HUMILITY AS A RELATIONAL VIRTUE

I remember one of my first interactions with Wendy, one of my very dear friends; she and I worked at the same institution for many years. During my first week at this new university, attending numerous new faculty events, my mind was flooded with countless new names, new ways of doing things, expectations others had for me, and expectations I had for myself.

At one particular formal luncheon with the university president and provost's office, I breathlessly walked in and saw Wendy, whom I had just met. She gestured me to join the person talking with her, introduced me to this person—who happened to be the provost—and listed several qualities and accomplishments about me with a warm smile and open face. This is something Wendy does on a regular basis with anyone; she looks for ways to include, uplift, and affirm those around her. She is also highly accomplished, quietly confident, and strategically discerning. She shows up to help, offer insight, and make space for others to do the same.

Here's the real beauty of humility: it's a relational virtue. Humility is not just about ourselves, not simply a personal virtue.

It is an *intra*personal and *inter*personal quality. A humble person prioritizes the needs of a group or relationship, rather than primarily focusing on the self. That is not to say they neglect their own needs, but they are aware of their own needs as well as others'. If they aren't aware of their own needs, prioritizing the needs of others becomes an unhealthy people-pleasing mindset. A humble person has the courage to identify their own needs, the confidence to keep those in mind, and the care to consider others at the core.

We see this in the experience of listening. I firmly believe we currently have a diminished listening epidemic. We've let efficiency and the priority of entertainment leak into relationships so people are primed to half listen. We half listen while on our phones, and while driving, calendar planning, vacationing, or making a meal. We half listen when we are more eager to be heard and to respond than to learn and understand. The humble person listens fully, to learn and understand. They are not guided by fear and insecurity, which so easily turns a dialogue into a monologue.

Humility rests on the premise that there's more to learn, which means seeking out the wisdom of others. But in survival mode, which is part of the initiating behavior of burnout, the focus is on the self. When we are in survival mode, when we are literally in a place where we need the most help, we're most often prone to avoid reaching out, avoid asking for perspective. Yet the idea that we should be able to "handle it" on our own is a lie.

Certainly we can be overdependent on others. In fact, the great error is either being too independent or too dependent. We talk a lot about this in communication studies. Being too independent means not knowing how to include others or work well with others. Being too dependent involves letting others rule your life and being unable to think or speak for yourself.

The happy balance is *interdependence*. This means having a healthy connection between autonomy (your sense of self) and connectedness (your ability to engage with others). Humility helps us distinguish between the extremes and find a place of interdependence by refocusing our priorities.

We are actually supposed to ask for help, not in a passive way, but in an apprenticeship way that seeks to learn and grow. James 1:5 tells us that we should ask God for help, who gives wisdom generously. Practically, God's help can be experienced through Scripture, the Holy Spirit, and godly counsel. For example, the Word of God points to Scripture as our source of guidance (Psalm 119:23; Matthew 7:24), and the Holy Spirit is called Our Advocate and our Helper and Counselor (John 14:26; Romans 8:16). We are also told to seek out wise counsel. Proverbs, known as the book of wisdom, advises us in 24:6: "Victory is won through many advisers." As you seek to grow in wisdom, what kind of advisors do you have? What kind do you want? How can you make that happen?

THE GRATITUDE KEY

Humility is so important that the Bible tells us we need to clothe ourselves in it, which means this is an intentional, everyday practice (Colossians 3:12; 1 Peter 5:5). This is a proactive process. In other words, we don't simply arrive at humility or grasp hold of it one time only. We have to pursue it daily.

Why is this so important in the context of calling? Remember a work calling involves a relationship with the Caller and community, and in order to have a close relationship with our Caller, and therefore a healthy approach to our calling, we need to take on humility. Taking on humility is hard to do, and we talk about the three specific ways this happens in chapter five. But first I want to introduce the foundation of humility, which is gratitude.

In terms of our calling, humility requires remembering where our calling comes from. Rather than passively responding to our calling, gratitude acknowledges the Giver. When we have gratitude for the skills, passions, and opportunities we've been given, it disrupts the temptation of pride, by focusing on the Giver rather than the self.

The other day, a friend of mine asked me, "How do you distinguish between recognizing the longing that exists in your specific calling, and being content? Saying, 'Wherever you lead me, Lord, I'm okay with that'?" That's a legitimate question. Too often we only see option one and option two. There's almost always a third option, it's just that the third option often requires us to live in tension, to balance the complexities, to recognize the nuance. If we are so focused on our calling, on the skills and passions we want to use, and we place the Caller in our periphery, then it's easy to feel resentment and self-pity. It's easy to miss the good and great opportunities that do exist.

At the same time, if we think of contentment as covering up our longings or dismissing them, we forget that the Caller is relational, we forget that he personally fashioned and developed us with these skills and passions, and he cares about us. Contentment is not passivity, it's an active recognition that just as we have longings, we can surrender them to the Caller and trust that he is on the move!

Within my circle of friends, I was one of the last ones to get married. Many of my friends got married in their early or mid-twenties. I found myself turning thirty, being single, and longing to the core of my being to have a life partner. I remember looking around at my other single friends who wanted to get married. They seemed to place themselves in one of two categories. Either they waited around for this partner to appear and didn't really live their lives to the fullest, or they denied these feelings and dove head-on into living their lives.

I tried to live in the third option: to acknowledge this longing I had to find my life partner, but also to start living fully. I traveled. I learned new hobbies. I kept pursuing my work goals, while also trying to keep my heart tender and ready. It was a daily process of active surrender. It was the ready acceptance of being vulnerable and living a whole-hearted life.

The same example could be used for a longing to be a parent or to find a meaningful work role. It's hard to live in the tension of the third option. It's much easier to harden our hearts and suffer resentment, or come to a standstill and refuse to move until these things happen. Humility requires us to live in the third option; tension and gratitude help us do this.

Gratitude is not a complacent, ambiguous, mindless type of acknowledgment, but an active, intentional, informed kind of giving thanks to the Giver of all good things. When we give thanks, humility becomes a superpower of sorts, and when approached well it can significantly alter our lives for the better!

What could this look like? We need to implement daily and weekly routines that carve out spaces to reflect.

The breath prayer mentioned in chapter two is one of the strategies I have implemented. When Colossians 3:15 pops up on my phone daily, I am reminded to "let the peace of Christ rule in your hearts since as members of one body you were called to peace. And be thankful." I breathe it in and out slowly as I read it. I let it rest in my heart and mind for a moment. I might ask myself, "Am I letting the peace of Christ rule in my heart right now?" or "How is the peace of Christ ruling in my heart?" I consider the ways God has helped me and cared for me. I breathe as I ponder these reminders.

This isn't a toxic positivity activity. This is a moment of noticing the little things, which over time add up to impact us in a truly and deeply positive manner. James Clear, author of *Atomic Habits*, suggests we focus on the small things, on 1 percent improvement, which over time adds up to big results.[8] In this way, he urges us to consider our trajectory, where we are going, rather than how fast we are getting there. He famously shares, "You don't rise to the level of your goals. You fall to the level of your systems."[9] If our goal is to be guided by sincere gratitude, then the way we approach our day, how we structure our time, and our focus impacts the gratitude outcome.

Another small habit, a newer system I've been doing for the past few years, is trying to go for a walk by the water once a week, on Friday mornings. For me, this is the day before I sabbath. It helps me have an anchoring, reframing of my thoughts and emotions before I make one final push in my work and then choose to rest. So for thirty minutes I walk in quiet and listen to the rhythmic waves and the birds making their morning music. It's incredibly grounding. It's often where I most feel the Holy Spirit move in my heart.

Another practice my family and I do is taking time each evening to share one thing we're grateful for from that day. My young son delights in this practice and always wants to know what Allen and I are going to say. Sometimes, his responses will be meaningful: "I'm grateful for you." Or silly: "I'm grateful for the trees, bees, and my knees." As simple as this practice is, it helps orient us. It's so easy to forget the good, when the hard is . . . so hard. We have to choose to remember.

A friend of mine, known for his dry and good natured but sarcastic sense of humor, gave himself a challenge of posting one thing he was grateful for each day for a year; he's not even on social media that much. However, for one year, he faithfully posted each day. It was impressive. A little while after this, he was diagnosed with colon cancer. In his mid-forties, with two young kids at home and a loving wife, this was a scary sentence. Chemo, radiation, and several ER trips later, he is cancer free. Throughout the cancer recovery process, I saw the impact of his gratitude challenge permeate his actions. His grit to get through it was bolstered by a new foundation of gratitude, to notice the way the Lord helped him get through it each day.

Once we are rooted in gratitude we are in a better position to locate and live out the virtue of humility, specifically as it relates to our calling. Let's pause and spend some time cultivating gratitude for what is good.

GUIDING QUESTIONS

1. First, let's consider mindset. In the last 24–48 hours, what have you been thinking about? What's been occupying your mind and heart?

   - *How* have you been thinking? Are you creating stories and adding narratives about yourself or others that aren't helpful?

   - *Who* have you been thinking about? And how have you been thinking about them?

2. Now consider actions. How have you been approaching all that's on your plate?

   - Have you been trying to do it all on your own? Why do you think that is? What's behind this?

   - Is there any part of what you're going through that could benefit from support or feedback?

   - If asking for help feels bad, why do think that is the case?

   - If you have asked for help but haven't received it, who else could you turn to? What other door could you knock on?

3. This chapter concludes by talking about the gratitude key and building in daily practices to take notice of people or things to be grateful for in our own lives. How can you make time to remember the good each day?

- What is one doable, manageable practice you can implement in your day or week?

ORIENTING PRAYER

Heavenly Father, Giver of all good things, thank you for being a relational God. Thank you for loving me when I'm messy and when I mess up. Thank you for wanting me to learn and grow. Please help me to notice all of the ways you are speaking to me now. Help me to notice the people you've put in my life. Help me to see the beauty you let me experience. Forgive me for the times I've let my calling overshadow my relationship with you, and with those you've placed in my life. I trust you. I trust you know me. I trust you are actively developing me. I give thanks for what you have done, what you are doing, and what you will be doing. I want you, my Caller. I seek you. Please protect me from distraction or discouragement. Please show me what it means to live humbly. Help me to walk this path with you at the center of my sight. Amen.

FIVE

PRACTICING HEALTHY HUMILITY

*P*inecones the size of a small cat. That was my first thought as I stepped out of the car and stretched my cramped body after several hours of driving. I had gathered with a small cluster of faculty who were part of a one-year group intentionally seeking ways to integrate faith into our academic disciplines, teaching, and research.

Set high up in the San Jacinto mountains near Idyllwild, California, a large cabin afforded a space to rest and ponder. Over one weekend, we were asked to make use of this idyllic, pine-scented piece of nature in order to connect with God. It was my second year at a university where I hadn't intended to stay, and I was missing what still felt like my home: Seattle.

That first night, I found a devotional on my pillow, which traced the story of Abraham and Isaac. It walked me through the unimaginable sacrifice God asked Abraham to make and the way out God provided once Abraham had surrendered. After reading this story, there was a prompt: "What is God asking you to sacrifice right now?"

I could feel my hand tighten in a fist and I looked down. *Home.* I knew it. God was asking me to surrender my sense of home, to trust where he had me. Mentally and emotionally, I couldn't pretend to be where I wasn't. I looked down at my closed fist and said out loud, "God, I won't lie to you or myself. I can open one or two fingers; would you please help me open the rest of my hand? I want to surrender to you completely, but I don't know how. Would you help me?"

That second year of being a professor, I received affirmation over and over again that this was where God had me. By the end of the spring semester, my hand was open. So were my mind and heart.

THE STRETCH BREAK

What do we know at this point? Like reaching for a sip of fresh, ice-cold water after exertion, living out your calling satisfies an internal thirst like nothing else. We know a work calling means work feels deeply meaningful, there's a relational pull from a Caller, we are able to apply particular skills and passions, and we feel like it makes a positive contribution among the community around us.

We know those who experience a sense of calling in their work often have greater work satisfaction, well-being, motivation, and overall psychological health than their peers. We know they are the people who impact others in a positive way, contributing to an overall increase in work productivity and a positive work climate. We know they have grit and resilience that inspires those in their community.

We also know that as motivating as a calling can be, there's a deceptive draw toward workaholism or job idolization, where the calling becomes toxic. In fact, those who feel called are the most susceptible to these dangerous shifts. With either addiction or idolatry we completely lose perspective and relationship—with ourselves, with our Caller, and with our community.

We also know burnout from a calling is a deeply disorienting experience, leaving collateral damage in some combination of shame, core exhaustion, mental paralysis, identity confusion, and spiritual disengagement, to name a few.

How in the world does someone who feels called—which is such a good, good thing—get stuck in burnout? That's where I don't want any of us to end up. What can buffer us, keep us accountable, and rescue us from the dark side?

Popular culture workplace experts who know the answer are really simply echoing what we can find in Scripture. The way to guard against burnout, the way to recover from burnout when it does occur, is not a self-made practice. It is not "seven steps you make." It is a different kind of surrender.

The way forward is humility. The way forward is modeled after the humility of Jesus. Philippians 2:5-11 describes how Jesus demonstrated this virtue, and beckons us to take up his model. Jesus wasn't confused about his identity, he knew who he was—the Son of God. Yet he willingly took on the flesh and bones role of a poor carpenter who socialized with outcasts, healed the filthy and unlovable, bravely spoke truth in the face of community peer pressure, literally washed the dust-caked feet of those he apprenticed, and offered his life through the most painful way possible so we might be co-heirs in the kingdom of God. Yet even Jesus showed an openness to learning as he sought his heavenly Father's direction in the garden, asking if there was another way besides death on the cross. And in the same breath affirming his trust in the Father's plan (Matthew 26:39). Jesus' humility is radical, reorienting, and redemptive.

His humility is radical because up until this point in history, humility wasn't really a virtue.[1] It's radical because he intertwined humility with love. Remember, there is no fear in love (1 John 4:18). Humility means we don't come from a place of scarcity; rather, we operate from a place of security. Jesus' humility is reorienting because it teaches us how to prioritize, and who and what to value. In his teachings we learn our mandate is to love—love God, love others (Luke 10:27). We learn the first shall be last (Matthew 20:16).

Our Caller's humility is also redemptive because it takes what is broken and heals it, restores it, and even elevates it. Consider the denial of Peter. After living with Jesus, learning how to follow him, seeing miracle after miracle, literally walking on water (and sinking), Peter's fear got the best of him. When given the opportunity to claim Jesus, fear took over.

What did Jesus do? After resurrecting from the dead, Jesus met Peter on the beach with a warm meal. Can you imagine doing that? After someone you love deeply betrays you, not once, but three times? Can you imagine making them a warm meal and seeking to affirm your love for them, after they rejected you when you needed them most? Jesus kindly helped Peter through a process of redemption by asking the question "Do you love me?" three times. Then, he offered Peter a role of shaping the early church. Humility redeems what feels impossible to redeem.

What does godly humility look like practically? How are we to model this kind of humility in our everyday lives, and how does it infuse our work calling with vibrant health?

Healthy humility involves three things: First, healthy humility means knowing your strengths and your weaknesses. In the field of communication studies, we call this *communication competence*. Second, healthy humility means being teachable, embracing an openness to learning. Third, healthy humility means knowing how to step away, delegate, take a break—to remove yourself from work and trust that it's going to be fine without you for a short time. This involves embracing the vulnerability of consistently taking time to rest and reflect; recognizing and acting on the strong belief that everyone needs refueling and to do well means rest is actually part of the process. Another way to think about the essentials of humility is this: know, learn, rest.

KNOWING YOUR STRENGTHS AND WEAKNESSES, AND NOT BEING DISTRACTED BY EITHER

Let's start with the first attribute. Healthy humility means knowing your strengths *and* your weaknesses. I had the honor of publishing some research about humility with three other amazing scholars, Bryan Dik, Don E. Davis, and Ryan Duffy, and we approach humility as the following: a relational virtue, involving an accurate view of self—not too lofty or too self-deprecating—and a focus on the betterment of others.

As I mentioned, in Christian circles we typically approach humility incorrectly. I'm not sure why this is the case. Perhaps it's like the game of telephone, where the original message gets convoluted as human beings listen and share based on their own filters and perceptions.

Scripture itself is very clear about what humility looks like and how we might seek it. For example, Romans 12:3-6 says,

> Do not think of yourself more highly than you ought, but rather think of yourself with sober judgment [the NLT says, "Be honest in your evaluation of yourselves"], in accordance with the faith God has distributed to each of you. For just as each of us has one body with many members, and these members do not all have the same function, so in Christ we, though many, form one body, and each member belongs to all the others. We have different gifts, according to the grace given to each of us.

Wow! There's a lot happening in this passage. Take a moment and read it again. What do you notice?

Humility starts with being honest with ourselves, about ourselves. Here again is the difference between modesty and humility. Unlike modesty, which can often be motivated by wanting to cover or minimize strengths, humility aims to make a true assessment of our selves. The key is *why*. Why is it important that we get to know ourselves? God made us. He made us in his image. He made us with purpose. Aiming for an honest view of ourselves must be rooted in trust in God.

We can't really be honest about ourselves if we do so in isolation. Identity formation is an ever-developing process. So as we seek to know ourselves, the most accurate way to do so is through the framework of who God made us to be. Therefore trusting in God as we seek to assess ourselves includes an awareness of the gifts God has given us, so that we can be a blessing to him and to others.

How can this be done? How can we both be aware of our weaknesses and our strengths, and also not get distracted by them? The way forward is gratitude. Gratitude gives us perspective so we are better able to see and know ourselves in light of our Caller.

A defining moment for me, in realizing gratitude is the greatest facilitator of humility, was right after finishing my PhD, during my first year working as a full-time professor at a university in Southern California. Being a Pacific Northwest girl at heart, I knew I felt called to this job for a time, but I wasn't sure I wanted to stay. I missed my family and friends in Washington. I wasn't altogether convinced the California vibe was for me.

However, in my second year, after having that talk with the Lord at the mountaintop retreat—after admitting to him that only some of my fingers were open, and asking his help to uncurl the rest of my hand—I won a university-wide award for teaching. The chair of our department at the time, Dr. Todd Lewis, surprised me with this news. As his face beamed at me, I distinctly remember lowering my head when he told me and offering a few objections, a few recent moments of failing. He said to me, with total kindness, "Don't do that. I see good in you. God gave you this gift. If you respond like that, you're insulting my opinion of your good work and the skills God gave you. Just accept it with gratitude." Accept the good things with gratitude, even when you feel undeserving.

It's weirdly hard though, isn't it? To let ourselves enjoy something we're good at? The key here is to remember Romans 12: the skills we have are God-given. These skills and passions aren't ours to begin with. The way to recognize strengths is to immediately turn it into gratefulness to the Strength Giver. Gratitude disrupts the temptation of pride. Gratitude acknowledges the Giver. More than that, gratitude focuses on the Giver rather than the self.

But what about weaknesses? How can we have healthy humility about our weaknesses? During a recent Christmas season there were a number of things that went wrong. One situation after another felt like hard hitting waves, and I couldn't catch my breath. Things just went from bad to worse, to even more so.

In the course of one year, we had some pretty serious health scares and diagnoses among multiple family members, two terrifying car accidents, and lots of other miscellaneous hard things. I specifically remember driving home and thinking, *Lord, I feel fragile.* I got an image in my head immediately of a potter's hands, soaked and caked with wet clay. I felt that Holy Spirit tap in my heart, saying, "It's okay that you're fragile. I'm the Potter, you are the clay. If you get too brittle, I can soften you. I can remake you if you break. It's okay to be fragile."

My friend, it's okay for you to feel fragile. Don't let that feeling distract you; you can turn it over to Jesus.

How do you do that? It may look different for everyone. For starters, try saying out loud, "Jesus, I can't handle this. I can't. But you can. I trust you. And I need your help." You don't have to carry the feeling of weakness like a mark of shame. Sometimes knowing your strengths and weaknesses also means being aware that even in your weakness his strength is there!

Listen, being consumed with our own weaknesses is just as damaging as being consumed with our strengths, because it keeps the focus on *ourselves* rather than God. Having an honest awareness of our weaknesses doesn't erase our strengths; it can allow for holy strength to enter in!

So humility is about thinking less of yourself (in the sense that you're not being distracted with yourself) versus thinking poorly of yourself (thinking badly of yourself).

Why does this matter? Because not being clear about what you're good at is like holding unopened presents and never really knowing what's inside. And not being clear on where you need to grow, what weakness you have, or being insecure and overly focused on your weakness is really just the other side of the same coin. It's pride; it's focus on the self. Healthy humility involves knowing what you're good at and approaching it with gratitude; it also means knowing where you need to grow and seeking God's strength rather than swimming in shame.

LEARNING AS A LIFESTYLE

The second component of humility is teachability, embracing a willingness to keep learning. I realize that I'm a professor and I work at a university where the whole point is to learn. Not everyone enjoys learning, and often learning can feel bad because it exposes what we don't know or what we currently lack.

Much like starting a workout after having not been physically active for a while, those first few weeks are not fun, painful even. Learning can be messy, but it is also part of what enriches life. Those who follow Jesus may call him many things (Shepherd, Savior, Healer), but one of the main titles given by his disciples is *Teacher*. Learning is part of the essentials in a life of faith. Now the key here is *how* you approach learning.

I was visiting my parents recently, and they asked if I'd go through a few old boxes. I came across some college papers they saved from when I was a student. Looking over the comments of professors, I found some that were mean, harsh, and frankly really unhelpful. Others, addressing the same kinds of errors, provided correction and direction but also kindness. It was definitely easier to be teachable in the classes where I felt seen and heard, in the classes I enjoyed.

It's definitely easier to remain open when things are going well, isn't it? It's much more challenging when you feel like a failure, or things get really hard. But humility involves being teachable even when it's hard, even when it's not fun.

This is also known as having a *growth mindset*. Stanford University research professor Dr. Carol Dweck is recognized for her work on fixed mindset and growth mindset.[2] These two different ways of thinking rest on one big difference: the view of failure. A *fixed mindset* involves the belief that you either have skills or you don't, and when you fail it's devastating. A *growth mindset* includes the belief that skills can be developed, and when you fail, you seek to learn from it and try again. Where do you fall in the approach to failure?

I'll be honest, failure is one of my worst fears; I can easily gravitate toward a fixed mindset. When I first realized how deep my fear of failure was, I wasn't quite sure where it came from. Growing up, in my home failure wasn't a shameful thing. Rather, the question was always: What did you learn from this experience? I did feel free to make mistakes. However, after taking a longer time to reflect, I realized I did have some experiences as a kid and teenager in school where teachers did not inspire that same sense of safety.

In elementary, I remember learning how to time my questions, or wait until after class to ask questions, so the risk of feeling shamed was lower should the teacher responded negatively. I'm mildly embarrassed to admit this, but there were some classes where the teacher's publicly unkind response prompted me to read a fiction book under the table rather than attempt the paralyzing math problem in front of me.

In fact, knowing firsthand what bad teaching can do and how it can influence learning, I initially resisted becoming a professor. Thanks to kind and very smart professors like Debbie Pope, Bill Purcell, Todd Rendleman, Renee Heath, Jeff Kerssen-Griep, and Christina Foust, my thinking was challenged in ways that didn't belittle me. Their feedback was sometimes hard, but always kind. They welcomed questions, and they knew how to artfully weave it into what they were trying to accomplish. They taught me how to embrace the intellectual playfulness of not knowing an answer to something and learning together in community.

Now that I have a child of my own, I try to respond to his questions with, "Did you know smart people ask questions? I'm so glad you asked that!" Part of being humble, part of embracing the health found in humility is knowing there's more to learn and welcoming the opportunity to do so.

Consider Psalm 25:9: "He guides the humble in what is right." Humility is a teaching process; guiding means going somewhere. Just before verse 9, the psalmist says, "He instructs sinners in his ways." God is humble and loving enough to want to help us. He wants to do this not because we deserve it, but because he is a loving, personal Caller. Not only does the Lord offer to guide the humble, he offers to walk with them, alongside them—he offers us his own way of learning.

Check out Matthew 11:28-30. Some of us have heard these verses before, but take a moment to pay attention to the role of humility: "Come to me, all you who are weary and burdened, and I will give you rest. Take my yoke upon you and learn from me, for

I am gentle and humble in heart, and you will find rest for your souls. For my yoke is easy and my burden is light." Jesus extends an offer to us, to learn from him because his yoke is easy and his burden is light. He invites us to learn from him and then tells us his heart is humble. He is modeling what it means to be teachable. So we don't have to have it all figured out on our own; he doesn't expect us to.

What's one of the primary ways we can demonstrate an authentic, teachable heart? We must guard against defensiveness. Humility involves a willingness to learn, to grow. Growth is messy, it requires perseverance. But it's not enough to start out with perseverance. James 1:2-4 prompts us to "let perseverance finish its work." Perseverance is enacted when we want to stop, when we are weary, but we know there is great good in continuing on.

In her book *Grit*, Angela Duckworth shares a story of an Olympic swimmer. In high school, this swimmer was over it. He was over having to get up incredibly early, swim, and train every day, over and over again. He told his dad that he wanted to quit, and his dad said, "Okay, you can quit, but *don't quit on a bad day*." If you choose to quit, quit on a day when you're not exhausted, you're thinking clearly, and you know what it feels like to win.

Even in the healthiest kind of work calling, we are going to have bad, sometimes really bad, days. We cannot let the bad days define and direct our next steps. And we are not alone in the bad days. The Lord is the best teacher and coach; we get to invite him to help us.

RESTING ON A ROUTINE BASIS

This leads us to the third part of true humility. Humility means knowing how to take a break. Walking humbly with God means vigilantly guarding and incorporating routine times of rest. This is one of those areas where it's easier to nod our heads and say

"Oh, definitely" than it is to actually do! It's much harder than we realize to let go, press pause, and walk away from the "tyranny of the urgent" for a set time.[3]

Here's what I mean: healthy humility recognizes that to function at our best means we need to rest. We are not the god of our universe; life will go on if we step away and rest. Taking time to sabbath means surrendering control to God.

Choosing intentional times of rest means trusting the Author of Time by tithing our time to him. Check this out. Hebrews 4:9-11 tells us: "There remains, then, a Sabbath-rest for the people of God; for anyone who enters God's rest also rests from their works, just as God did from his. Let us, therefore, make every effort to enter that rest." What do you notice here? We are encouraged to make every effort—not if it's convenient, or simply feels good— but to make the effort, regardless. It doesn't say perfect rest. It says make the effort to rest.

Earlier I shared that I've come from a recent season in life that was exceptionally hard. Every week I found myself practically crawling on my hands and knees toward the Sabbath. My family and I sabbath together on Saturdays. It's not easy, but it's *always* worth it. Inevitably, every time sabbath arrives, my mind gets flooded with work I should do, things I can control. But making the effort to sabbath releases me from the seductive lure of workaholism and pride. It helps me see that in the midst of all of these hard situations God has been faithful, and my surrender is part of that process. Ruth Haley Barton, spiritual director and cofounder of the Transforming Center, reminds us rhythms must be intentionally formed; they don't happen by coincidence. Sabbath creates a rhythm for humility to enter in.

For my family, part of our sabbath rhythm includes sabbath pancakes and intentional prayer time. We might add other things like a run along the beach, a hike in the mountains, or some fun, life-giving activity. Regardless, we have our pancakes and our prayer time.

When I was thinking about how to make sabbath prayer time a little different, a little more focused, one of my mentors suggested a particular meditative prayer called the prayer of examen.

There are five steps to the prayer of examen:

1. Ask God to bless you with graced understanding (e.g., Lord, help me to make sense of what's going on).
2. Review the day in thankfulness.
3. Notice the feelings that surface.
4. Choose one of those feelings and pray from it.
5. Look toward tomorrow, and conclude with the Lord's Prayer.

This can take five minutes or thirty. It can be done alone or with someone else. However you choose to approach it, it's worth it!

Remember, rhythms are established through intentionality. What kind of new rhythm can you enact that might help you rest? Rhythms help us insert times of reflection, which are the seeds for healthy humility. When we take time to reflect rather than skim social media, when we take time to reflect rather than binge-watch a show, when we take time to reflect rather than keep ourselves so very busy, it gives us an opportunity to cultivate a heart of humility. We need to dial down the noise.

Sabbath helps us examine where our strengths are and take time to thank God. In times of rest, we can examine where our weaknesses are and invite the Lord's strength. We can examine where we've felt like a failure and choose to learn from it and keep on going. Or, as Dory from *Finding Nemo* would say, "Just keep swimming. Just keep swimming. Just keep swimming."[4]

Sabbath does require practice, but sabbath is the practice of the humble. It isn't easy to do. There's always a reason to postpone it. It's often uncomfortable because we live in a culture that thrives on being busy. It is always, always worth it to stop.

In our third year of marriage, Allen and I traveled to Taiwan for a family member's funeral. We traveled in the middle of July, which means thirty seconds after getting out of the shower we'd be covered in droplets of wetness again from the humidity. One afternoon we needed some welcome cool air and a moment to catch our breath, rest our hearts. We took the subway to a place that served high tea at the top of a building with a breathtaking view. Holding our soothing tea, sampling sandwiches and scones, we sat in silence for a while, letting our weariness surface in a safe space.

We started talking about what gives us rest. And suddenly a light bulb went off for both of us. We realized, as it relates to feeling restored, I am more of a contemplative person who finds restoration in nature and in slowing down. My husband is more of an active person, who feels rested from doing fun things. So on a paper napkin we charted out how to start integrating both of these elements into our sabbath. For reference, Gary Thomas's book *Sacred Pathways* really helped us understand these qualities about our own spiritual rest.

Here's a pro tip for sabbath: have a pre-game strategy. Consider the day before you try to sabbath and the day after. What might need to be adjusted? Where might you need to work harder on the day before or after so you can unplug on a true day of rest? We have to be proactive about rest rather than reactive. We must pursue it before we need it rather than waiting until we are desperate for it.

We need to get comfortable with a term called *sabbath sadness*.[5] Researchers and theologians have found that when we take time to slow down, all of the things we've been keeping under the surface rise in the stillness. It can make us feel deeply sad, and sadness is something we are often uncomfortable with, something we see as a problem.

One of my favorite Pixar movies, *Inside Out*, wrestles with the role of joy and sadness, ultimately helping us see how necessarily intertwined they can be for our development. Chronic sadness is debilitating, taking us deeper into places of despair and depression. However, healthy sadness can prompt us to seek comfort. It can also reveal unknown thoughts and feelings we need to address, or even help us shift certain choices and actions we didn't realize needed adjusting.

Sadness can be scary, or at least not pleasant. When we let ourselves feel sad, we open ourselves up to pain, feeling a loss of control. But remember, emotions are like tunnels; we need to go through them to get to the other side. What if we allowed a little bit of sadness to surface long enough to explore why we are feeling that way, what contributed to it, and what the sadness might be leading us to?

STEPS FOR THE HUMBLE

In the bright light of calling, it can be hard to imagine feeling burned out. And yet, those who feel called are the most prone to burnout. How can we protect ourselves from being overcome, or how can we recover from burnout? Seek a life of humility. What does this mean? Healthy humility involves three things: know, learn, rest.

First, know your strengths and your weakness. We need to take the vulnerable step of examining skills God might be developing in us. What areas of strength and passion may be surfacing? We also need to reflect on where we might be distracted with our own weaknesses. Are we focusing on internal stories of weakness that blind us to other parts of reality? Are we so distracted by what we think are gaps that we can't move forward? We can invite the Lord to fill the gaps. Invite him to help us look up and look out.

Second, be teachable with a willingness to learn. Start with questions like "What am I facing right now that could be a good learning experience if I humbled my heart just a bit? Is there a situation where I've been a little defensive or where I want to quit because I feel like a failure?" We can invite the Lord in to teach us how to learn from him. Sometimes this does mean walking away from something, especially if it's unhealthy or harmful. But if we know deep down it's a worthwhile thing, and we're just tired, we must let perseverance finish its work. Let's not confuse an opportunity to learn with what feels like finality in failure. We are children of God and he has invited us to learn from him.

Third, consistently take time to rest and reflect. The very best thing we can do to cultivate healthy humility is to build in regular times of rest. We lose perspective when we are weary. Everything looks worse and feels worse. We should pursue sabbath like we'd pursue the love of our lives, because sabbath is an act of love. It is not only tithing our time to the Author of Time, it's the practice of releasing control and seeking the Lord's presence. It is the willingness to feel awkward and messy because resting isn't a normal practice, but doing it because we know that this is what the Lord has asked of us.

Our Caller has shown us what is good, what is actually expected from us: "To act justly and to love mercy and to walk humbly with our God" (Micah 6:8). The Lord encourages us, requires us in fact, to walk with him. He tells us that we can do this by being humble.

GUIDING QUESTIONS

1. Revisit the story of God asking Abraham to make an unimaginable sacrifice in Genesis 22:1-19. How might you answer this question: "What is God asking me to sacrifice right now?"

   - Or, if you're in a season of not feeling close to the Lord, try this question: "What's something I need to let go of that is of great value to me, but may in some way be holding me back? What do I need to let go of?"

   - Consider holding out your hand. Don't force it—be honest with how much you can open up your hand and allow that physical sign of surrender.

   - Then ask God for help to give it fully over to him. Consider telling someone you trust about this and asking them to check in on you as you seek to let go of something, to make way for what might be better.

2. Recall the first attribute of humility—being aware of your strengths and weaknesses, but not distracted by either one. What's an area where you currently feel weak, an area where you feel lacking, and possibly even overly aware of your own faults?

   - Maybe this area of weakness is becoming an all-consuming thing. You don't need to stay in this place! Invite God into that weakness right now.

   - Try saying, "Father, I need your help." Try saying it a few times, not because God needs to hear it more than once, but because you do. Ask the Lord to fill the gaps for you. You can trust that he will.

3. How we were treated in the past has the ability to direct our present focus. When you think about experiences in your life that shaped your approach to failure, what stands out?

   - What experiences shaped your approach to learning?

4. For the second attribute of humility, teachability, is there an area in your life where you might benefit from being more teachable?

- Where are you feeling weary in the learning process? Invite the Shepherd in; you don't need to learn on your own!

- Invite the Lord to be your teacher. Ask him to show you how to learn. Learning from the Lord brings rest for your soul.

5. In the third attribute of humility, making rest a routine, we see the value of slowing down and taking a breath. Developing a routine time of sabbath is key to this. What kind of rhythms do you currently have in place?

- How are they impacting your life?

- What's one rhythm you'd like to start?

- How can you begin this process in the coming week?

ORIENTING PRAYER

Lord Jesus, thank you for being the best teacher. Thank you for wanting me to learn. Thank you for being patient with me as I keep learning. Please forgive me for any area of my life where I have been trying to take control or idolize success over growth. I want to walk with you. I want to learn the rhythms of your grace. Savior, help me know how to approach the strengths and skills you've given me in a healthy way. Show me what it means to keep learning in this season. I want to rest in you. Protect me from distraction as I seek to rest. Show me how to rest well in you. You are my Caller, and my calling is yours to do with what you will. I surrender to you. Amen.

PART THREE

THE WAY FORWARD

SIX

BOUNDARY SHAMING
AND BOUNDARY RESILIENCE

Philosophical poet, theologian, and social critic Soren Kierkegaard famously said, "The thing that cowardice fears most is decision."[1] On a good day, I feel pretty confident about decision-making. My dad often jokes about praying to God before I was born that I would have an innate strength for making wise decisions. Usually I can see the layers and implications and offer strategic thinking that yields positive outcomes. However, I've learned that one of the worst times I make decisions is when I feel backed into a corner, whether it's a time-pressured scenario, where every second counts and we're already behind, or when someone else's urgency screams at me or my own weaknesses feel glaringly present. If I'm not careful, an internal chaos rises, kicking my decision-making into survival mode rather than feeling centered in my role, purpose, and pace.

When we think about burnout, particularly calling burnout, we have to address the connection between burnout and boundaries. Boundaries are what help us make and follow through with good decisions. We have to do this on behalf of ourselves and in consideration of others. Boundaries are the guardrails on the road of a healthy calling.

With more than 75 percent of people reporting experiences of burnout, it would be fair to assume we'd want to support each other in avoiding and recovering from burnout, wouldn't it?[2] Some of us might be familiar with particular workplace terms based on the impact of more recent waves of burnout, like the Great Resignation and the Great Disengagement.[3] One key question we need to ask is, Why are people getting to this point? I don't think it's any one thing, although wouldn't that make it easier? And in our time, I'm not attempting to answer the bigger, more meta why.

I do think there's something to address with those who feel called and are feeling *calling burnout*. Here the focus is less on the *doing* and more on the *being*. We need to attend to our identities and the way they are being pulled, stretched, distorted, and even manipulated.

One of my mentors, Elizabeth, manages hundreds of employees, but has the art of making each one feel seen and heard. While meeting with her, I was explaining my tension of feeling caught between knowing what healthy work boundaries are and feeling the strain of organizational change, social crises, and more work to be done than there are workers to do it. Especially among female colleagues and friends, as research reports, there is massive overwork.[4] They are navigating full-time work, with kids at home and/or caretaking for aging parents, pushing themselves beyond their comfort levels in an unsustainable manner. The result of this push includes a growing cynicism toward work that once felt like a gift. I did not want to get to that point.

Elizabeth nodded her head. She leaned forward and said, "In recent meetings we are starting to call this the duplicity of two messages." As a communicator, I felt like this new phrase turned a light bulb on for me. Yes! That was exactly what I was feeling. Here's what the duplicity of two messages sounds like:

Take care of yourself, but work more with less.

Pursue mental health and rest, but fill in the gaps because we are understaffed.

We need you to do more because all of us are sacrificing.

The duplicity of two messages means we are simultaneously being told two competing, often opposing messages at the same time, with the expectation that we do both.

I was so bothered by this that I decided to make a list of five women I respected in both their professional and personal lives, and ask them how they managed the tension of caring deeply about their work but also live a balanced life. I contacted each one individually, asking if I could treat them to coffee. I came with specific questions, made notes, and thematically analyzed their responses (because as a researcher, I can't help myself, even if the data set is N = 5). I asked them things like: How did they do it? What lessons had they learned in the hard times? Check out the themes I found:

1. *It's a season.* It is only a season if you intentionally make changes when possible. Otherwise, it becomes a lifestyle.

2. *Make time for yourself.* This is really only an option if you take the risk of being judged for it and know some things will suffer; but it's still the right choice.

3. *Declare the values in your life.* You need to know what they are, and you need to have the courage to communicate them when needed.

4. *Believe what you're choosing to do is legitimate.* This means not letting others define what success looks like for you in the context of your life.

These are amazing lessons, aren't they? Certainly, it's easier to think about this when we're feeling clearheaded and lighthearted.

The problem is, when we're tired, when we're on the road to burnout, it's much too easy to feel confused, apathetic, and even
shameful. Shame blinds us. Shame causes us to stop hearing
truth. Shame is a silencer. Shame is what convinces us to hide in
the dark.

Before we aim to turn the lights on, I want to sit with you for a
moment. I want to sit beside you. To do that, we need to get really
clear on the type of shame that comes from calling burnout.

DEEP SHAME AND VULNERABILITY

Part of what distinguishes burnout and calling burnout is the role
of shame. For calling burnout, shame is often central, strong, and
deep. We may be somewhat familiar with the word *shame*, but
what exactly is it and why does it matter so much? One of the
great contemporary voices in the conversation about shame is
best-selling author, professor, researcher, and speaker Brené
Brown. In her famous 2010 TED talk, "The Power of Vulnerability,"
she addresses what she calls "the silent epidemic" of shame. She
describes shame as intense, painful feelings of being unworthy of
love and belonging.[5]

Shame can cause us to hide (emotionally, mentally, spiritually,
and/or physically). Shame prompts us to lash out in hurtful ways
to others because of the pain it brings. Perhaps most significantly,
shame completely disorients us from what is true. Shame convinces us to continue down a bad road because we literally feel
beyond repair. Shame blocks us from seeing any possible sign of
hope, redemption, or possible change from the current torment
by which we feel consumed.

Let's take it a step further—shame from calling burnout is what
experts might call *deep shame*. Deep shame is consuming, evident
in a chronic sense of unrelenting worthlessness, self-doubt, mag-
nified inadequacy, and immense self-disappointment.[6] Why does

burnout from a calling often permeate on a deeper level, creating a sense of deep shame, more than typical work burnout? It has to do with identity and relationship.

When calling burnout occurs, resulting feelings of shame can distort our relationship with the Caller, convincing us we are wasting, destroying, or even violating the skills, passions, and opportunities our Caller has given us. That is deep shame. If our calling is no longer meaningful to us, if it feels like an overwhelming and hopeless burden we are no longer capable or desirous of carrying, it disrupts what we have come to know of ourselves and we feel ashamed of ourselves. That is deep shame. And if we cannot continue to live out our calling, we can also feel like we are harming those who could be positively impacted by it, letting them down and perhaps even causing (perceived) harm to others. That is also deep shame.

What do we do? Brown suggests shame is the strongest when it remains unspoken.[7] With this in mind, the first step is to admit those feeling to ourselves and to someone we trust. Brown calls this *being vulnerable*. Her solution is actually to embrace the messiness of vulnerability rather than believe the lie we can somehow compartmentalize this shame.

It is vulnerable to admit that what felt like a sacred gift in our calling has shifted to a suffocating burden. It is vulnerable to reconcile when we must say *no*, even though we see the need is great and we feel the urge to respond to the need. It is vulnerable to pause the momentum of our calling, to surrender the schedule, pace, and tasks that seem so important, so we can rest. A healthy calling is vulnerable.

I remember hearing Brown's talk for the first time and then devouring all of her books. I was in my doctorate program, trying to compartmentalize all of the stress and challenges such a season included. I learned feelings of deep exhaustion and chronic stress can't be locked in mental and emotional closets for long. At some point, they impact the rest of our physical, mental, emotional, and spiritual space. As God's amazing timing would have it, this is also the same season I began the hard and the priceless journey of routine sabbath.

Learning how to live and lead with vulnerability is indeed a life-changing lesson. In the pursuit of having healthy vulnerability, there are good days with easy wins and there are harder days with difficult losses. But we have to take the first step, and there's a companion to vulnerability that helps make this possible: boundaries.

THE UNDENIABLE CONNECTION BETWEEN SHAME, BOUNDARIES, AND CALLING

Renowned pastor, author, and speaker Charles Spurgeon famously said, "Learn to say no. It will be of more use to you than to be able to read Latin."[8] Spurgeon's comment may not be a catchy mug meme or T-shirt text. Nevertheless, I want to post this somewhere public and present, to remember it as often as possible! Saying no might feel limiting, but in the right circumstances it's really empowering.

Learning to say no to good things so we can experience better things may sound easy, but it can feel really hard—hard to know when it's the thing to do, and hard to do it. Yet there's a healthy vulnerability that comes with saying no. The healthy, vulnerable *no* means we say no to something that feels controllable or certain in exchange for what may seem unknown or unclear—but it is the better choice. It means we risk disappointing others so we do not disappoint our integrity.

The healthy *no* means we took time to consider the long game, the bigger perspective, and we see the value in doing the right thing over the immediate thing. It is much easier to have this kind of vulnerability when we are clear on our boundaries.

Two expert voices about boundaries are Henry Cloud and John Townsend.[9] Partnering together for decades in various writing and speaking projects related to boundaries, Cloud and Townsend, both of whom are best-selling authors, psychologists, expert speakers, teachers, and leadership consultants, are best known for their iconic book called *Boundaries*.[10] Their research suggests boundaries involve drawing a personal line between who we are and who we are not, based on the values and goals we have for our lives. We must each be responsible for setting and safeguarding our boundary lines.

Boundaries protect what is valuable, and boundaries free up what is meant to expand. As it relates to our calling, boundaries keep us grounded. Having healthy boundaries with our calling means we recognize the great value, the actual gift, of having a calling. When we do this, we're motivated to care for it with a bit of awe, like a priceless treasure. Healthy boundaries also provide direction for what's actually worth striving toward and what is not. Healthy boundaries are the enactment of wisdom, being able to say no to some things, even very good things, so you can say yes to great things.

So a quick review: Shame is dissolved when we prioritize vulnerability. An accurate understanding of vulnerability is done best in partnership with boundaries. Boundaries keep our calling in a place of reverence. How do we actually do this? How do we have boundaries with something that feels like a holy compelling, with a deep and visceral pull?

Here's where humility makes this easier! Humility positions boundaries as essential rather than optional.

Consider the first aspect of humility, having clarity on your strengths and weakness, and not being consumed by either. Humility frames boundaries as a necessary way of keeping balance, of staying afloat. To protect our strengths from taking over in a prideful way, we have to learn to say no when the opportunity simply strokes our ego, potentially feeding a godlike complex or addiction. To be aware of our weaknesses and allow space to grow, we have to learn who or what helps and hinders this process.

I'm grateful to have opportunities in my work. On the occasions when I'm asked to speak, write, consult, or guest lecture in seasons where my plate is already quite full, I can be easily tempted to say yes. After all, these opportunities appeal to my sense of calling. However, they may not be necessary or essential. If I'm only saying yes because it feels good to be seen, needed, or honored, I have learned that's not a good enough reason. I am familiar with the dread and regret of saying yes to those things and feeling the strain on my calendar and in my relationships.

On the flip side, if I'm given an opportunity to speak, write, consult, or guest lecture but the reason I am tempted to say no is because I'm overly aware of my weaknesses, that's not a good enough reason. I remember being invited as the keynote for an all-staff conference. In that season I did have the time, but I was afraid. I was afraid I couldn't fulfill their needs, afraid I wouldn't achieve my own ideals in the given context. At the same time, however, I felt the Lord begin to form a specific message in my heart for these employees. I'd be driving in the car or getting ready for the day, and part of a message would land in my mind; I'd have to stop and write it down. So I said yes and surrendered the desire to do my best in exchange for the desire to honor the Lord with whatever he had for me.

In fact, when I was first approached about writing this book, I said no, primarily out of fear. I had a two-year-old. I was working full time during a time of institutional and societal change in the aftermath of a global pandemic.

After being asked a second time, I took a day to really pray about it. I laced up my tennis shoes and went on my waterfront beach walk, glancing at the feathered clouds against the glowing blue, feeling the tingle of sweet cold wind and warm soft sun. I stood at the curve of the path, looking at the ebb and flow of sparkling waves, watching young families exhilarate at the wonder of the ocean rhythm. And I felt the Holy Spirit's whisper in my heart: *If the only reason you're saying no is out of fear, that's not a good enough reason. Lean on me. Take the risk. Trust in me.* I asked my husband if he was willing to journey with me in this, knowing if I said yes, it would impact my family. He was and is one of my biggest encouragers. I asked two or three other people I admire for their counsel. They all supported this choice. So I said yes. And here we are!

Second, humility as a mindset of lifelong learning means sometimes we succeed and sometimes we fail, yet we openly learn from both circumstances. In this way I have to constantly pursue a growth mindset, because it doesn't come easy to me. I naturally feel drawn to being intimidated by my own failures, letting them define me and take me out. Yet, I have learned to take these concerns to those I trust. I have learned to wrestle with and then shake off previous moments that felt less than my best. I have also learned who I should not process my thoughts and feeling with, even if they are my friends; their approach may not work for me. I have learned to be selective in my teachers of life. Having good counsel is invaluable to learning. Boundaries help us choose who we should learn from and who we should not.

Lastly, to learn well we must make time for reflection, the third aspect of humility. Boundaries buoy this value by helping us carve out space for reflection. Humility embraces the need to take a break, to remind ourselves we are not the god of the universe.

This partnership of humility and boundaries also helps us learn how to keep pursuing designated times of rest even as it's hard to fully enact. We are so bombarded with busyness, so conditioned to multitasking our way through life, it's hard to allow our bodies, minds, and hearts to rest. We also rest in different ways. Some of us recharge by contemplation or relaxation. Others feel rested by seeking purposeful play, partnering with people or projects that feel life-giving. In whatever way we might experience it best, routine rest absolutely requires boundaries and is sustainable through humility.

We have to learn when to say yes and no. Feeling bad about saying no isn't necessarily evidence it was actually a bad choice. Recognizing when other people are unconsciously or consciously trying to shame us into ignoring our boundaries is key. That is an important step in the healthy calling process.

BOUNDARY SHAMING

A major contributor to the harmful cycle of burnout is boundary shaming. I define *boundary shaming* as "the act of someone (often a person with power or influence) imposing their definition of work and their personal capacities on us, in a way that that makes it appear unacceptable to say no." Certainly, we are expected to fulfill our occupational requirements. But boundary shaming is beyond what's actually expected of us. It's when we are pressured to conform to another person's work capacity standard, and if we do not we are seen as "not being part of the team." Negative consequences could include being passed up for promotion or work opportunities, or even job termination. If we do conform, we do so at the potential cost of interpersonal relationships and harm to ourselves.[11] Boundary shaming may not be intentional, but the impact still happens.

Many well-meaning individuals assign their own capacities on others, especially if the work feels hard-won. As it relates to those in power over us, I've often thought there are two types of leaders: leaders who lead from their pain and personal trials, who expect us to go through what they went through, because they did; and leaders who lead from the lessons they've learned, aiming to help others avoid unnecessary pain and hurdles.

Boundary shaming can be hard to spot initially, often happening progressively. For example, my friend Anne accepted a job at a nonprofit, with the promise from her new boss he would quickly promote her, based on her qualifications, and modify her current role to one more specifically suited to her skill set and passion. It would just be a few weeks before that happened. After two months of doing what felt like menial tasks she didn't agree to, and being asked to overwork on a regular basis, she requested a meeting with her boss. She asked for a timeline about role shifts and was told, "We're all doing things we don't want to do. And we have another candidate we're considering for the role you want. So we need you to prove yourself just a little bit longer." She waited another month. Nothing changed. Another meeting, same response. This is the point where she and I met.

Anne and I talked through the options, and she realized this job was not only absent of meaning for her, she felt taken advantage of and shamed for trying to form healthy work boundaries. Realizing she could get sucked into this job with no promise of future meaningful work, she decided to quit. She texted me right after this, saying she immediately felt a sense of peace and relief, despite future uncertainty. This was not an easy choice for her, especially with school debt to consider. However, she reached out to her network of work contacts, and within a month she was offered a position that not only appealed to her skill sets and passions more directly, the work culture itself was collaborative and honoring.

I checked in with her recently, and her response was, "Things are going really well. I feel super grateful! I feel like I'm starting to settle into a rhythm at work and I love it. Everyone's really welcoming. It's been busy, but really good. I'm excited to see what's to come." If Anne had allowed herself to bend to the boundary shaming of her first boss, she would have missed this opportunity.

Boundary shaming makes its dangerous appeal by targeting what we value most: relationship. Whether it's the relationship with our Caller, the community we seek to impact, or even our own sense of self, boundary shaming in a work calling happens when we attempt to draw a line between our work and the rest of our lives. But the person imposing their own definition of work and level of capacity challenges this line, implicitly or explicitly bringing to question whether we are fully committed, capable, and/or caring.

In academic circles we might label this as intentionally or unintentionally commodifying our calling. To *commodify* means to inappropriately try to market, sell, or make money out of something that was not intended for that kind of use. When someone commodifies a person's calling, they minimize our personal boundaries for the sake of an organizational or relational gain. For example, "We know you value being home in the evenings for your family, but this [insert work thing] is the only time we can do it. We know you've already been working longer hours, but we're under pressure to get this done quickly."

This type of communication on an occasional basis may be part of work's ups and downs. However, if this becomes a regular response when questions are raised about working extra hours or hours we did not originally agree to do, then it deserves a pause.

When this happens, we need to give ourselves plenty of space to reflect. Remind ourselves what our actual calling is about. Remind ourselves of our work and life goals. Remind ourselves what boundaries make us feel good and healthy, and then, and only then, let ourselves respond.

We need to come from a place of mindful evaluation rather than pressured time, heightened emotions, and anxious scarcity. We might have to say yes to what's less than ideal—that's not what this is addressing. The concern is when the very thing driving us is used to harm us. Friend, let me just say, I have learned and am continuing to learn how to do this well. It's an ongoing process, and it changes as our lives change.

After having my son and returning to work, I remember a season of choosing to say no to what felt like extra work events and opportunities in order to be home with my young family. Yet, I also felt the strain of judgment from those who would not have made that choice. Even other women with children, who had either different capacities or priorities than I did.

Once my son started preschool, I mistakenly thought I could re-prove my commitment by taking on extra roles and tasks for a short season. The result? Those looking to judge my commitment were never satisfied; it was never enough for them. Those who knew my work calling commitment were already on board, affirming and supporting me. The other result? I was tired and unsatisfied, human Swiss cheese, feeling stretched with holes. I felt like I wasn't doing anything particularly well.

One particular morning, I remember driving in the car with my husband. He asked me, "What percentage of your work currently feels like a calling?" Normally, it's about 80-85 percent.

I paused and really took stock of how I felt and what I was doing. I faltered in reply as I realized the answer, "I . . . I guess, I guess about 40 percent."

"That's not good," we both said at the same time.

No, it wasn't. So over the course of a few months, I made some adjustments, said no to some nonessential or "no longer working" commitments, and opened up space for more of what brought me joy.

If we allow the commodification of our calling and accept the boundary shaming as normal, then we run the risk of workaholism, job idolization, manipulation, and/or exploitation. This is why those who identify with a work calling are more prone to burnout than others. The relational responsibility to the Caller and community can easily blur boundary lines. We forget the *why* of our calling.

It might start out as giving into one request, and then another, and another. One day we wake up and realize resentment has taken the place of joy, cynicism has taken the place of believing the best in others and ourselves, and exhaustion is no longer seasonal but normal.

The commitment to work and these toxic calling approaches have a strangely similar appearance. But chaos has no place in a healthy calling. There may be storms, but peace can prevail in storms. Chaos implies lack of order, lack of intentionality, lack of care. Chaos is purposeless. Calling is purposeful.

What can be done about this? We must guard our sense of self and the why of our calling so fiercely that even if others in our community are choosing to do it differently, we are secure in the knowledge of our choices. If you're feeling chaos, that's a sign to pull over. Take a break. Get some perspective. Working harder won't dissolve the chaos. Pursue rest; fight for it if you must.

BOUNDARY RESILIENCE

Boundary resilience is the opposite of boundary shaming. It is led by humility, which means we are open to changing what isn't working, and we are clear on where we draw the line between what feels healthy and what is not. Boundary resilience means learning to adjust boundaries when necessary, maintaining them (even if we feel like we are failing), and asking for help when we realize we cannot do it alone. In the following chapter we'll talk about two practical ways this might happen. For now, let's explore this wonderful quality further.

Boundary resilience is not the same as quiet quitting. The basic idea of *quiet quitting* is when people put in the very minimum amount of effort to do their work and avoid any sense of going the extra mile. Yet our work doesn't just impact us, it impacts those around us, those who may be causing the overwork, and also those we simply work alongside.

Organizational experts have varying beliefs about whether quiet quitting is good or bad. Here's what I'd like to suggest: quiet quitting can be harmful if (a) we try to dull down our calling and/or (b) our quiet quitting harms those around us. Work is rarely an individualized thing. If we stop doing the work, who will suffer? If it's someone who is not causing the initial harm, we should take a long pause to consider whether quiet quitting is simply an inverted way of seeking control when we feel out of control, at the expense of someone else.

Boundary resilience requires courage. It means we stop apologizing for the boundary lines we create. Henry Cloud gives a great template for articulating healthy boundaries that goes something like this: "I understand my decision might feel upsetting and it isn't what you wanted to hear. Other than changing my position, what can I do to help?" Boundary resilience originates in humility because the goal isn't about getting it right or wrong. Rather, the goal is to keep learning, keep growing, all the while holding to what we value most.

So what can we do when we experience boundary shaming or calling burnout shame? What if we tap into what New Testament scholar Te-Li Lau suggests about the potential of shame?[12] Lau suggests shame can be formative in a good way. Reaching the path of burnout can be helpful if it causes us to take account of why and how we got there. If we can be accountable for the decisions we've made and the decisions we need to make moving forward. In Lau's perspective, shame doesn't have to be the handcuffs we often feel it to be. Burnout does not have to equal failure. What if, as TikTok therapist Kobe Campbell suggests, burnout is an opportunity to realize the way we've been living is no longer sustainable, based on what we have learned and the new boundaries we need to develop?[13]

Here is where the relationship with our Caller comes into play. It's not that he called us once, he is continually calling us. The thing about having a dynamic, ever-growing relationship with our Caller is that Jesus is not just in the business of saving our souls. He's concerned about the salvation of our emotions and our minds, too. Consider Mark 12:30-31: "Love the Lord your God with all your heart and with all your soul and with all your mind and with all your strength." This command does not stop there, it's not just about one relationship in one area; it's about what this one relationship means for all areas of our lives.

Pay careful attention to the completion of this command: "Love your neighbor as yourself." These are partner commands. Our Caller is concerned about the salvation of our souls, our emotions, our minds, and our relationships. To love this way requires humility. To live this way requires humility. To experience a healthy calling in this way requires humility.

My friend, there is nothing, nothing more satisfying than connection with the Caller, Jesus Christ. When it comes to talking about meaningful work, work that feels like a calling, that's good, even great. But it pales in comparison to unity with the Caller. Whatever thirst you're feeling, the only one who can truly quench it is Jesus, not just individually, but also Jesus within our community.

Perhaps you've found yourself in a toxic calling, wrapped and twisted up by what used to feel like good goals and responsibilities, but now feels more like an impossible burden. Perhaps you've made choices you knew were not good, not actually motivated by a sense of calling but rather pride or people-pleasing, choices that have hurt those you love, choices that have hurt you. These don't have to be what keeps driving and defining you.

If the joy that sparked your mornings is now just dull, sour smoke and ash, it doesn't have to stay that way. God is in the business of redemption. He redeems with delight. He rescues with whole-hearted love. He continues to create with holy genius and a desire to name what he creates as "good." Fear lies to us with what feels deceptively like reason and truth, getting us to hold tightly with a closed fist to things out of a feeling of scarcity, the fear of not enough.

It's time to let go.

The Caller may be asking you right now to uncurl your fingers, and you don't even have to do that alone. Ask him for help. Ask your trusted few for help.

Be brave enough to slow down and reflect on what's working and what's not. Choose small goals, based on larger value systems, and revisit them each week for a period of time. Change can happen, but change won't happen if we just keeping passively waiting. We must actively wait. Actively waiting involves participation and preparation in what might happen. It means being ready. Being ready could involve more training, new habits, more networking, or letting go of what feels easy and familiar to make space for what you'd like to see happen.

My friend Lucy recently shared she was afraid of wanting a work opportunity that fits her perfectly but isn't what God has called her to in this next season. I looked at her, as I would look at you, and said this: That fear makes complete sense. But remember God is a relational Caller. If he is truly calling you to something that you don't currently want and you keep your hands open to him, one of three things will likely happen: he'll gently change the desires of your heart to align with where he's called you; he'll let you experience this other option to realize for yourself that it's not actually what is best; or he'll provide a new alternative that's better than what you currently see. God cares about your interests and skills because he cares about you.

And the good news is that he's not motivated by simply what would please you; that would make him a servant. Instead, he's motivated by what is best for you because he created you and loves you with great care. If you daily trust him with your dreams, they may not turn out the way you wanted, but you will see the hand of God in new ways that will bring you a joy you didn't think was possible. The Caller is worthy of your trust.

GUIDING QUESTIONS

1. As you think through ways of integrating work-life wellness practices into your own life, which of the following four practices stand out to you?

   It's a season. Remember it is only a season and intentionally make changes when possible. Otherwise, it becomes a lifestyle.

   Make time for yourself. This is really only an option if you take the risk of being judged for it and know some things will suffer but it's still the right choice.

Declare the values in your life. Know what they are, and have the courage to communicate them when needed.

Believe what you're choosing to do is legitimate. This means not letting others define what success looks like for you in the context of your life.

2. Another way to think about work-life wellness pursuits is this: On your best, most rested day, which of those practices seem doable, seem actually possible to bring into your life?

   - Similarly, when you're the most run down, carrying the heaviest weight, feeling the most stretched, or at a total standstill, which one stands out to you?
   - Why do you think that is?

3. Consider the last few weeks. Is there a task, opportunity, or person you should have said no to because it caused you to feel overextended?

   - Is it possible to return to this situation and alter your commitments, without causing harm to others?
   - If not, what can you learn for next time?

4. What would happen if you made it a goal for the next week to ask for more time to respond before saying yes to something else?

   - Even if you give yourself thirty minutes to think it over, make it a goal to add margin to your decision-making process for the next seven days.
   - Then, evaluate how that process went. What else might you need to tweak?

ORIENTING PRAYER

Abba Father, Great Redeemer, thank you for loving me even when I feel unlovable. Thank you for forgiving me even when I feel unforgivable.

Thank you for offering me new mercies each morning, even when I feel like I've worn out my welcome. I want to learn how to create healthier boundaries in my work and in my personal life. I need your help. I want your guidance. I want to make sure my calling remains sacred and my relationships are life-giving. Help me not to succumb to people-pleasing and pride. Help me to stay alert to the sliding and slipping away from my boundaries. Remind me what my goals and priorities should be. May what I do, and what I seek to do, be glorifying to you, my Caller and my King. Amen.

SEVEN

OIL AND FRAMES

I think it's fair to say that as a society, we're mesmerized by new fads promoting wellness. We follow, like, love, post, share, and repost what feel like doable steps that promise feeling better, looking better, being better. Lotions and creams, various types and amounts of water, the newest diets, exercise routines, and sleep support—advertisements, tutorial videos, and influencers offer "the thing" that's going to change our life for the better. Thousands upon thousands of articles make note of ways to improve. Some of these fads offer new and fleeting insight, while others pull from ancient practices wrapped in new packaging. For example, articles like "11 Best and Worst Oils for Your Health" offer new tips and tricks to make the most of oils that help cell growth and protect your organs.[1]

Yet historically oil (e.g., olive oil) has long been referenced as "liquid gold."[2] Practically, olive oil was used for lighting lamps, healing dry skin, and cleaning wounds. Metaphorically, oil symbolized fruitfulness and vitality.

There's something communicatively sacred about the application of oil, for the one applying it and the one receiving it. In Christian theology, oil is part of anointing or designating a person or place as holy. For example, in Psalm 23:5, David writes of the Lord, "You prepare a table before me in the presence of my enemies. You anoint my head with oil; my cup overflows." In Hebrews 1:9, we learn how Jesus is set above all others:

"Therefore God, your God, has set you above your companions by anointing you with the oil of joy."

Oil is also linked to the attributes or presence of the Holy Spirit, such as in 1 Samuel 16:13: "So Samuel took the horn of oil and anointed him in the presence of his brothers, and from that day on the Spirit of the Lord came powerfully upon David." In Isaiah 61:1, the Spirit of the Lord is referenced as anointing Isaiah, and then again in the New Testament, Jesus refers to this verse in Isaiah as he declares in Luke 4:21, "Today this Scripture is fulfilled."

Recognizing the symbolic role of oil matters for us in our exploration of a healthy calling because the virtue of humility is referenced as a type of oil. Research suggests humility is in fact good for you and good for those around you.[3] In our case, humility is a kind of metaphorical oil expressed in a healthy calling.

THE SOCIAL OIL HYPOTHESIS

We've been spending some time looking at how humility helps guard and rescue us from calling burnout. Let's talk about what this means in action. There's actually a psychological term for the positive attributes of humility.

Notable psychology professor and scholar Don E. Davis suggests humility functions as a balancing agent, a way of keeping internal and external harmony. Davis and colleagues coined this phenomenon the "social oil hypothesis."[4] Their research points to humility as social oil, protecting and enhancing personal and professional relationships. How exactly does it do this?

The social oil hypothesis sees humility contributing to a healthy professional and personal life in three specific ways, which can directly be applied to work calling: balance between our self-concept and others; clarity between personal work calling goals and larger, primary calling; and a refocus on relational priorities in both work and personal life.

First, humility helps balance our concern for the needs of the self and others. Unlike modesty, which might not highlight an awareness of self but simply defer to others, humility is about knowing ourselves fully (strengths and weaknesses) while also being mindful of the needs of others. Instead of being a doormat (overly dependent) or an island (overly independent), humility helps us remain interdependent. Humility keeps burnout at bay by drawing a boundary line between ignoring the self or being consumed by the self and a healthy sense of self.

Humble people who feel called are comfortable apologizing, but not wasteful with apologies. If we're operating from a place of humility, we know when to apologize but also how much to apologize. A humble, healthy calling does not include wallowing in mistakes; it does include addressing them. This also means we've allowed ourselves time to reflect on an interaction that didn't sit well rather than ignore it or be consumed by it.

My son attends a physical activity class after school once a week. This class teaches kids how to listen well and operate as a team by providing obstacle courses and games for them to work through. Initially the tasks are easy, then they make it harder to see how the kids respond. Do they give up? Can they think through alternatives? Some of the main goals of this process are applying self-kindness, using critical thinking, and embracing perseverance. One of the mantras the teachers use is "Practice makes progress." I love that! Practice makes progress.

Shame attached to calling can make us feel like we're failing when we're not able to do what we feel called to do. But if we remember it's not about perfection, not about perfecting our calling, rather it's about improvement, growth, and sometimes starting over, we are making use of humility's social oil. So before we move on, would you say it with me? "Practice makes progress."

Humility embraces this truth, freeing us from fearing our weaknesses or focusing too much on our strengths.

Second, humility as a social oil helps balance our view of work as a calling and the larger purpose of our life. Humility keeps us grounded by reminding us of the greater perspective. When we do that, we don't run the risk of forgetting who the Caller is, we don't mistake ourselves as the god of the universe. We remember this calling is not the definition of ourselves, it is the expression of ourselves. We remember the process part of calling, the way it grows, develops, and even changes.

Humility helps us pay attention to the long game rather than only the immediate urgencies. This is especially important during an economic crisis, organizational shifts, or heightened seasons of stress. Humility helps us stay mindful of what we have learned in the past, what we are learning now, and what we can learn for the future. It helps take the pressure off of having to perfect or control what's in front of us, by keeping us mindful of the larger goals. Sustained stress acts like horse blinders, diminishing our ability to see ourselves and others well. Like 20/20 vision, humility helps us see close up and far away. To do this well, we need time for reflection.

One of the best ways we can allow humility to take over, to act as what Tennyson calls "the highest virtue, the mother of all of them," is by routine times of rest and reflection. But here's the thing about routine rest: when we slow down from a breakneck speed, we often become aware of negative feelings we didn't allow to surface at such a fast pace. Enter *sabbath sadness*, that thing we talked about in chapter five.

Because I'm a big promoter of sabbath and I mention it frequently in my classes, students often make office hours with me to discuss it further. Over the years, some patterns have emerged. One of these patterns is articulated in responses like: "Sabbath doesn't work for me. When I slow down, I feel sad, like uncomfortably sad." Sabbath sadness is when all of our thoughts and feelings we've attempted to compartmentalize over the week crash into us like hard waves. The result includes feeling lonely, melancholy, more tired, or even depressed. So then we might think, *Sabbath isn't for me. I don't want this feeling.* In these times, we need to remember, feelings are like tunnels we go through.[5] Sadness can actually lead to something else. It does not need to be the destination.

Now, sabbath sadness has been discussed a bit by theologians; it is characterized by a feeling of deep internal aching, uncomfortable sorrow, or encompassing melancholy brought about by slowing down. I'd like to suggest there's another kind of problem we might experience in a pursuit of routine rest: *sabbath survival.* We live six days of our week at crazy, chaotic speeds, running hard and fast and then falling into sabbath, expecting one day to somehow refresh us from six intense days.

If that's a rhythm you've been trying, it's actually just perpetuating a survival mode, or boot camp mode, unsustainable in the long term. In this scenario, we're not really approaching sabbath as a day of relational connection with our Caller, with a mindset of reflection and restoration. Instead, we're using sabbath as a day of basic recovery.

What we should be doing, what invites humility as a social oil, keeping the balance between work calling and life purpose, is *sabbath surrender.* Sabbath surrender takes into account what we need to let go of during the week so we're not just a shell of ourselves when we get to a dedicated time of rest. Sabbath surrender keeps our hands, heart, and mind open for what the Caller may need to communicate to us on a day dedicated to this mindset. Sabbath surrender is a letting go rather than a fizzling out.

When I first learned how to drive, my dad had me sit in the driver's seat and asked me to locate the gas tank information. He pointed to the red line and said, "Don't ever let it get to the red line before you fuel up. Once you're at a quarter of a tank, pull over and refill." He went on, "It's an issue of safety. You might think you have time to fill it up later, but you never really know what's going to demand your attention. Build margin in your tank. That way your response isn't being dictated by urgency."

Now, I realize there are several memes about the "two kinds of people" who let their gas tank get to a quarter of a tank versus all the way to red. Frankly, I'll be honest and say I don't understand the latter and I'm married to one! Yes, in some ways the actual gas tank scenario might be a personality issue. The difference, however, is we are not machines. If we let ourselves get to the red line, our consequences involve flesh and blood, important relationships, and personal well-being.

As it relates to rest, let's be on guard about getting to a place where we're running on empty, sick from stress, and motivated by scarcity. Let's create some burnout boundaries by pulling over when we notice we have only about a quarter tank left of compassion for others and ourselves, energy to keep going, and the ability to think holistically and creatively.

Sabbath surrender is not waiting until the tank is empty to get it filled. It's pulling over with margin to spare. And when we take time to do this, we won't have the whiplash effect of six hard days and one metaphorical hospital day. We'll have the impact of six meaningful, possibly hard days, and one day of sanctuary.

Lastly, humility as a social oil helps us balance our work goals with our professional goals by emphasizing the prosocial (other-oriented) quality of calling. Humility helps us avoid job idolization that positions work as the ultimate priority. When we succumb to this form of idolatry, we use the excuse of our calling to defend our actions and hurt those around us. Humility helps avoid workaholism, which positions work as the great fix. When we think of work as the main thing that will bring us happiness and fulfillment, we use the excuse of our calling to traffic bad habits in our lives. Humility keeps our work in proper perspective. It helps us remember the people in our lives are also worth treasuring, caring for, investing in, and loving well.

Humility helps us balance our work goals with our relational goals so we aren't living an overextended life. In caring for a healthy calling, we cannot let chaotic schedules take over and suffocate our patience. If we remember to focus on our Caller rather than being fixated on our calling, we live life with open hands rather than tightly closed fists. Humility protects us from using our calling as an excuse not to show up for those in our lives. Humility reminds us our calling is about relationship with our Caller, our community, and ourselves.

HOLY HUMILITY

As we explore humility further, one thing to consider is the inability to fully be humble on our own. Really, what we're talking about here is holy humility, humility we cannot possibly obtain by ourselves but can experience only with the help of the Holy Spirit.

The truth is we need God's help to be humble; the good news is he offers it readily. We see this in 1 Peter 5:6-7: "Humble yourselves, therefore, under God's mighty hand, that he may lift you up in due time. Cast all your anxiety on him because he cares for you." We are urged to humble ourselves under God's mighty hand, to come under the authority of the Lord in order to take on humility. One version of this Scripture says: "So be content with who you are, and don't put on airs. God's strong hand is on you; he'll promote you at the right time. Live carefree before God; he is most careful with you" (MSG). One way to think about the distinction between humility and holy humility is considering to whom you're surrendering.

Holy humility involves peeling back a deeper layer of surrender. It isn't just a mindset of choosing not to dwell on our strengths and weaknesses; it's an awareness of God's role and his promise, as in 2 Corinthians 12:9: "My grace is sufficient for you, for my power is made perfect in weakness." Holy humility isn't just a desire to keep learning, an awareness that we don't know it all; holy humility recognizes God as our teacher. In this way, we look and listen for his guidance on a daily basis. Holy humility isn't just the practice of taking a rest each week, and it is certainly not what some call "self-care Sunday." Holy humility is the desire to follow God in all our ways, including his practice of resting. It is a longing to pull away and re-center ourselves by intentionally seeking the presence and company of our Lord.

When we accept the loving authority of God in our lives, we experience full humility. There is no security like the security of being faithfully loved. If you've forgotten you're faithfully loved, if you've never really let yourself believe it, now's the time to make a change. Now is the time to truly consider the calling you've felt in your soul. This calling comes from the Caller, and he is a personal, loving God who made you with intentionality and who cares deeply, deeply for you.

This is the backbone of humility: when we remember we are loved by the Caller, we can offer love to ourselves and to others. Humility as a social oil is most powerful when we remember whose we are.

COMMUNICATION FRAMING

What really excites me about the application of the social oil hypothesis with regard to humility and a healthy calling is that we can start making these changes right now in our communication (with ourselves and others)! When we learn how to talk about our calling in a certain way, it gives us better tools to set limits on work demands. Communication researchers Fairhurst and Sarr originally coined the term *communication framing* after over ten years of research at a multinational organization where they saw how certain managers were able to thrive, despite unusually stressful work situations, specifically based on how they framed their experiences and their roles. How did they do this? Through intentional communication practices, which require conscious listening, focused attention, and perspective taking.

Communication framing is the ability to actively listen, mindfully engage in discussion, offer and invite feedback, and embrace problem solving discussions with the goal toward conflict resolution or relational care.[6] It requires taking time to think about what we are doing and why we're doing it, and then communicate this to ourselves and others. In fact, Fairhurst and Sarr noted that those who are able to think ahead about how they might respond to situations had significantly higher, more positive responses than their peers.

When being asked to ignore or overextend your own work boundaries and capacities, some examples of communication framing might include:

- For those in your personal life who may not understand your work calling, "I get to go to work. I really love what I do and am grateful for this opportunity. I look forward to telling you about it when I get back" (instead of, "I have to go to work," and then not sharing what you've done). Here, there's a direct reminder of work feeling like a gift and you're wanting to share it with those around you.
- For those in power over you at work expecting more of your time, "I'm really committed to this calling in my work

and what we're doing here. If it's helpful, here are the times I am free [insert times]. I want to perform at my best, which means being consistent with planned times of rest and recharge with my family (or personal community). Rest is part of what makes work life-giving." Here, there's a balance of knowing what you're allowed to say and how to say it. Framing work as a priority by connecting high performance to rest is key.

- For those who work with you or for you asking for time with you, "It's my joy to meet with you [person at work]! I will have to conclude our time by [insert time, so you have margin before the next meeting]." (Then consider setting a timer so you can fully focus on that person but also have a third-party reminder to end.) When you're clear on your time boundaries at work, you can be "all in" during those times without regret. It also gives the other person a sense of value and clarity of expectations.

In order to apply this well, we have to take time to slow down and reflect. This is why a primary part of the success of communication framing hinges on the third quality of healthy humility—the ability to let go and take a break for a while, to choose rest as part of a healthy work approach. How do we do that? We need to build in (sometimes fight for) routine times of self-awareness and empathy.

The chaos and cacophony existing in the Western culture normalization of burnout makes it hard to hear our own thoughts and stay connected to our own feelings. Communication framing strategies recognize that what we say impacts what we believe. It includes prioritizing time to realign what has become out of whack, to move from boundary shaming to boundary reclaiming, resulting in boundary resilience. From this posture we avoid shallow cynicism, which seems to protect us but really depletes us of experiencing meaningfulness amidst the imperfection.

This communicative framing isn't just about how we talk with others, it's also about how we talk with ourselves. We need to be mindful of our own self-talk. In burnout, it's easy to get lost in an echo chamber of messages about failure and lack of worth. It's easy to keep chewing on mistakes and regrets, so by the end the actual scenario has lost all original meaning, form, flavor, like an over-chewed piece of gum. One way to help those lies diminish is to find someone who knows us well and can speak the truth to us. This may be a spouse, a friend, or a parent. It could even be an author or podcaster who we feel speaks words of truth to our very core.

Music is a mood-maker for me, a perspective rudder steering my thoughts and my feelings. During my most recent pull into burnout, I was in the middle of getting ready for work, heavy in heart, absent in mind, and sluggish in body. And then I heard CeCe Winans singing: "They say this mountain can't be moved. They say these chains will never break. . . . You are the way when there seems to be no way. We trust in you, God, you have the final say."[7]

This well-known singer reminded me of who I am and want to be. She reminded me of who my Caller is and how he feels about me. I had this song on repeat every day for a week, sometimes super loud and singing alongside her in my car with the full depth of my lungs, sometimes very soft with the only other movement being the splash of tears dripping down my face. Her lyrics helped me communicatively reframe my calling.

When we apply the idea of framing to our calling, it gives us *agency* (autonomy, the ability to act freely). It gives us the opportunity to consider how we are talking about our calling, how we are experiencing our calling, and how this might be leading us down the sticky path of the dark side of calling, of workaholism and job idolization.

Let's peel this back a bit more. Consider what an unhealthy calling might sound like:

"I need to do this. If I don't do this, it will get dropped or won't be done well, or we won't make the kind of impact we should. No one else can do it the way I do it!"

"This is my calling; I have to say yes to this project. It's important. I know my plate is already full, but just this one more project and then I'll take that break I've been talking about. Just one more yes."

"If I don't do this project, no one will. It will get dropped, and I really care about this."

"If I don't do it, it won't get done right. It won't land well with the people I'm trying to help."

"If I don't do it, the people who can be positively impacted by this won't be helped. I can help them."

Allowing humility to reframe your calling might shift the narrative to:

"This new project does make use of my strengths. I really want to do it. But do I have enough energy left to add this to my plate? Will my sleep and relationships suffer? Am I saying yes because it will feel good to be a part of this or because I know it's the right time and the right thing to do?" (The humble calling recognizes our strengths and weaknesses, and isn't distracted by either.)

"If I say yes to this, what will I say no to? Can someone else do part of this work? Who can I ask for help who has the skill set for this? Who might even benefit from getting a chance to take this on? Even if it's not done the way I would have done it, can the goal still be achieved?" (The humble calling is teachable, willing to learn and delegate.)

"I am sensing that I'm pushing too hard, for too long. On the one hand, I'm sure I could keep going, but if I do, I won't have any margin room left. In fact, I was impatient with my spouse for the tenth time. My own child had to tell me I was on my phone too much. If I trust that my Caller will provide another way, I need to show that by releasing control. I need to take a break. Not later, now." (The humble calling knows when to take a break, knows they are not the god of the universe, and recognizes the value in routine times of rest.)

What did you notice? One glaring commonality among both sets is the tendency to do more, often connected to a prosocial pull, which is part of the makeup for those who feel called. We feel the need and want to respond to it. Other approaches to work (e.g., job or career) might find it easier, or even more desirous, to say no. Yet framing calling with humility redirects the need. It moves from a desire to respond to the pull of the calling, to a desire to honor the Caller.

What's incredible about communication framing is when we talk about our work, we hear ourselves too. Like one of the examples above, I've found myself shifting from "I *have* to go to work" to "I *get* to go to work" when telling my son why I was leaving for a meeting. When we come from a place of humility, we frame our calling with the mentality of lifelong learning. This means opportunities aren't seen through the scarcity model, with questions like "What if nothing like this comes along again?" Because then we say yes to more and more and more. Instead, we take a moment to consider "Is this the right time to say yes? Do I have enough resources left to give it my all?"

Humility also helps us frame calling with a balanced perspective by holding to our calling convictions with a mindset toward how it impacts ourselves and others. By allowing humility to partner with us in our thoughts and our actions, we are ensuring that our Caller is leading us, rather than the calling or the community.

It's hard to say no when the options are all part of what we love to do. It's hard to say no when we aren't the ones in power and those who have power over us are adding very real pressures. It's hard to say no when the consequence may be opportunities delayed or missed altogether, for ourselves and for others. It's hard to have the courage to frame our calling to those who may not understand or respect it.

Learning how to frame our calling is a process. We aren't meant to do it alone. We often need others to help us. And it doesn't happen overnight; it's not a one-time deal. It's part of calling maintenance.

My friend, open the door to the echo chamber and let the lies out. You don't need to house them anymore. Let the fresh air in. Your Caller is calling you. You may feel like you've lost your way; you may have. However, he knows the way out.

GUIDING QUESTIONS

1. Sabbath sadness and sabbath survival are two things to pay attention to in our pursuit of healthy calling and rest. Knowing sabbath sadness isn't necessarily a bad thing, what's one practice you could incorporate into your next time of rest, to help you through the tunnel of sadness, to get to the other side?

   • How might you give yourself space to do this well?

2. Similarly, knowing sabbath survival is not what rest was intended to feel like, how could you structure your time in other

parts of the week, so your day of rest isn't a "junk drawer" for dumping everything else you didn't have time to do?

- How might you incorporate a different time for errands, important tasks, and events so your actual time of rest is protected?
- What's one thing you could do the next time you pursue rest?

3. When you think about the idea of sabbath surrender, what's one thing that's getting in the way of you pursuing rest like this?

- What do you have control over?
- What do others have control over?
- Take a moment, right now, to look at your calendar and carve out 1-2 hours in your coming week. Whether it's a walk or journaling at a coffee shop, find time for whatever practice helps you internally slow way, way down. If you can't this week, go to the next week—find a time. Write it down. Don't wait until next month. Move things around if you must, get up earlier if you must. Clean your internal framing mechanism in your heart and mind so you can properly view your life.

4. Return to the examples of unhealthy calling versus humility-framed calling. Which list felt more familiar to you, for your own life?

- From the first set of narratives, in the unhealthy calling, which example felt most familiar to you? Why do you think that is?
- For the second set of narratives, in the humility-framed calling, which one stood out as something you sense you should be saying, or want to say?

5. We aren't meant to pursue a work calling on our own. When you think about ways to change the communicative frame, who can help you find your frame for a healthy calling?

- What voices do you need to seek out to help you realign the way you talk about your calling?

- What voices do you need to silence that belittle, disregard, or diminish your calling?

ORIENTING PRAYER

Lord of lords, King of kings, I want you to be the King of my heart. I want your voice to be the voice I hear. I want the way I talk about my work to glorify you. Help me have the courage to talk about it in that way. Help me find the voice I need, to speak about what makes the work I do feel like a calling. Grant me favor in the eyes of those I work with, with those in my life, so that they might inquire about my calling, and in replying to them I may glorify you. Artist of artists, design my calling frame so that as I talk about it to others, as I listen to my own self respond, you further paint the picture of my calling. Help me to keep growing. Help me to stay surrendered to you. Freedom giver, the place I want to be is at your feet, on your path. Amen.

EIGHT

THE WAY FORWARD

I'm still learning.

The other day I said yes to a work commitment I shouldn't have. Perhaps I was primed from earlier stages of work life when saying yes to most professional opportunities is usually a good thing. At this point in my career, that wasn't the case. I could feel myself coming down with a cold, but the invitation was something I wanted to do. It was something I cared about, although not essential. As soon as I agreed to it, I felt that feeling. You know the one? I felt a little anxious, irritated, drained, foolish, and stressed. So I turned to my humility checklist:

- Did I make this choice with an over focus on my strengths (wanting to show them off) or my weaknesses (wanting to prove I could somehow "do it all")? *No, that wasn't it.*

- Did I make this choice because I wasn't open to learning? I didn't want to delegate? *No, not really.*

- Did I make this choice because I was operating from a mode of scarcity? Was I so caught up in the motion of a chaotic schedule that I said yes without taking time to reflect and consider my boundaries and current capacity? *Yes. Yes, I was doing exactly that. Bummer.*

I confess, I felt ridiculous for falling again to this lie, this deceitful lull of workaholism that whispers, "It's just one more thing. You'll make a difference. You can do this. It's not that much extra time."

I started to spiral toward shame, not wanting to share this because I should know how to make wise choices by now, shouldn't I? I'm writing this book, I'm sharing lessons from personal and empirical data. Shouldn't I have learned this by now? Ah, there's where the inverse of humility number one *and* two, pride, started surfacing. I was embarrassed of my weaknesses. I was annoyed at myself for still needing to learn this lesson, again.

The bright side? Here's where the internal muscles started showing up. All of these thoughts happened within five minutes. I found a quiet space in my home. I held out my hands and said to my Caller, "Lord, I'm so sorry I didn't pay attention to how I was feeling. I was more mindful of my calling than my Caller. Please forgive me. Help me to learn from this. Show me if there's a way to return to the person and say no without causing undue harm to relationships or work progress." Within a few hours, the person I had said yes to contacted me, unsolicited, and said I was released from this time. She'd find another time later.

Immediately peace flooded my heart and mind. But it doesn't always work out that smoothly. I'm sharing this with you, my friend, because as we're nearing the end of this particular conversation, I want to remind you that what we've been talking about isn't a five-step guarantee to avoiding burnout altogether.

This isn't an easy recipe for *always* having a healthy calling. Practice makes progress, not practice makes perfect. What we've talked about, what we've covered, is the dynamic process of living out our calling in such a way that we can aim to avoid burnout. And if somehow it takes over, we are able to get out. We are not stuck. We are not defined by burnout.

THE NECESSARY RHYTHM OF REMEMBERING

The word *remember* in Scripture is used 352 times, and if we include the same meaning found in similar phrases, like *don't forget* or *keep it close to your heart*, it leaps to over 550 times.[1] What's so wonderfully human, so significantly humbling, is that the students who sat at the feet of Jesus and witnessed miracles firsthand needed to be reminded, often. Why would we think we are any different?

We will always need to be reminded. Needing to be reminded isn't the problem. The problem is when we resent or deny the need to be reminded. The problem is when we aren't allowing humility to be our compass to help us manage calling burnout.

If calling burnout is a manageable problem and not necessarily a fixable one, how do we move forward? What is the *way* forward?

A work calling includes experiencing meaningfulness in our work, identifying a Caller, using our skill sets and passions, and positively impacting those around us. Let's not go too fast past this review. When we review these four categories again, what stands out? Of the four elements in a work calling, is there one that feels specifically dim right now, perhaps close to burnout?

Meaningfulness. Have you lost a sense of meaningfulness in your work? Has the sense of meaningfulness grown a bit fuzzy or dull? Do you find yourself doing things that seem more functional, heavy on the task mode, light on the meaning? Is there a monotonous, robotic routine where there used to be fresh joy?

Caller. Are you feeling far away from the Caller or, worse, does the Caller feel far away from you? Sometimes it is easy to forget this whole calling experience is about relationship. If you're feeling alone, let me assure you these feelings do matter. They do! However, feelings are only part of reality, only part of the story. Take a minute to remember: What do you know to be true? What has been true for you in the past?

We are told in Psalm 34:18 that God is "close to the broken-hearted." In fact, our Caller wants to be so close to us that he isn't afraid to gets his hands dirty, as we see in Psalm 147:3: "He heals the brokenhearted and binds up their wounds." In his invitation to draw near there's a personal hospitality promising a safe welcome. If you feel far away from him, know this: your Caller is standing at the door, knocking.

Skill set plus passion. Does it feel like your skills and passions are not being used, or you've sort of dried up in your capacities? Or has something happened to the type of work or approach to your work, diminishing that feeling of using your core passions and skills? You've taken on more, but the kind of more that does not feed your calling. Remember, busyness suffocates meaning, empathy, and perspective.

Positive impact. Are you feeling like you don't matter or you can't make a difference anymore? Perhaps it feels like the positive impact on others isn't really happening. Too much hardship in the world at large, or in your own community, seems to have eclipsed the good you used to see. Part of what brings illumination is the willingness to engage in reflection and then act on it.

Which of these areas might need some fresh air? How might this happen? Consider some ways you can communicatively frame your calling right now. How might you apply the pursuit of humility here? If you don't know, the first step is to locate a sense of gratitude, our key to humility. This is not a complacent, ambiguous, mindless type of gratitude. It is an active, intentional, informed kind of giving thanks to the Giver of all good things. Gratitude is the heart of healthy humility.

HUMILITY REVISITED

As we've talked about, healthy humility involves three key components. First, humility means knowing your strengths and your weaknesses. Consider for a moment: What strengths might God be developing in you right now? Or where have you recently been distracted with your own weaknesses? Invite the Lord to fill the gaps. Invite him to help you look up and look out. We aren't supposed to live static, unmoving lives. We are meant to live dynamic lives, which means growth is good and in fact necessary.

Second, humility involves being teachable, having a willingness to learn. What are you facing right now that could be a good learning experience if you humbled your heart just a bit? Is there a situation where you've been a little defensive, or where you want to quit because you feel like a failure? Invite the Lord in to teach you how to learn from him. Sometimes this does mean walking away from something, especially if it's unhealthy or harmful. But if you know deep down it's a worthwhile thing and you're just tired, let perseverance finish its work. You are not a failure! You are a child of God and he has invited you to learn from him.

Lastly, humility means consistently taking time to rest and reflect. The very best thing you can do to help cultivate healthy humility is build in regular times of rest. We lose perspective when we are weary. Everything looks worse, feels worse.

Pursue sabbath like you'd pursue the love of your life, because sabbath is an act of love to the One who gives life and who is actually Love. It is not only tithing your time to the Author of Time; it's the practice of releasing control and seeking the Lord's presence. It is the willingness to feel awkward and messy because resting isn't a normal practice for us these days. We pursue it because we know this is what the Lord has asked of us.

Burnout can be completely disorienting. When we don't know the way forward, we can look to the One who does. If we can't see him, we keep looking. For he has shown us what is good. He delights in continuing to show us. What does the Lord require of us? We know from Micah 6:8 that he asks us to "act justly, love mercy, and walk humbly." The Lord encourages us, requires us in fact, to walk with him. He offers to be the light when we cannot see the light. He tells us we can do this by being humble.

Compassion fatigue, quiet quitting, the great resignation, the great disengagement, quiet firing, empathetic distress—all of these are reactions to being overstretched, overstimulated, manipulated, perpetually exhausted, or overtaken by a scarcity mindset. In this broken world, there may not be a way to fully protect ourselves from these things, but there is a way to not be overcome by them.

The healthy calling realigns us to our sense of purpose and our sense of impact. Humility keeps our calling healthy. Burnout boundaries are part of humility's reframing.

BOUNDARIES BOUNCE BACK

Wouldn't it be nice if we could make immovable, unchanging boundaries? Maybe it's the list lover in me, but I would be easily moved by the potential to select boundaries, make them, and then never have to think about them again.

Breaking boundaries and flexing boundaries are not the same. As we consider boundaries and communication framing, it's more about paying attention to our current goals, situations, and people involved. We can often achieve our goals in multiple ways while still keeping our boundaries. However, it does require using discernment and having courage in the way we frame our work calling boundaries, depending on the interactions.

It takes courage to slow down in the midst of hurry. It takes courage to reject cynicism in times of uncertainty, to stay focused on our actual goals rather than what we may be feeling in the moment. It takes courage to have hope when it leaves us feeling vulnerable and weak, to live in the tension of the in-between.

A great model of having the courage to slow down is found in Mary, the sister of Martha and Lazarus. In Luke 10:39 we are told there was one sister, Mary, "who sat at the Lord's feet listening to what he said." Mary's choice to slow down wasn't laziness; it was goal clarity. She proactively sat at the feet of the Teacher. Essentially, she came right up to the front of the class, to actively, unapologetically listen and learn.

When we have the courage to slow down, we make space to discern our priorities. Sometimes we don't realize fear and worry have become the guides to our decision-making, until we slow down. When we slow down, we also notice other people better. It's hard to be kind when we are in a hurry, when we are overly stressed by doing too much.

This is hard to do! The movie *A League of Their Own* gives a fictional account of the real-life All-American Girls Baseball League formed during World War II.[2] There's a particular scene when the coach, played by Tom Hanks, faces a player about to quit the game. When she says that it just got too hard, he says: "It's supposed to be hard. If it wasn't hard, everyone would do it. The hard is what makes it great."

Even on a good or great day, a work calling can feel really, really hard. We may feel the pull to help more, do more, be more. We may see the need so clearly it's hard to shake it from our thoughts. We may be wrung out by the end of the day, from giving and giving and giving. Let's take a lesson from Shel Silverstein's book *The Giving Tree* and not turn into a stump.[3] We cannot keep giving if we aren't ourselves growing. We cannot keep growing if we aren't replenishing.

With that in mind, what if some of our prayers start including things like: "Lord, help me to discern when and how to slow down. Grant me the courage to slow down and trust you, even when everyone else is rushing by."

When we use communicative framing to help create boundaries for a sustainable healthy calling, we also protect ourselves from being overtaken by cynicism and a hardened heart. Hardening our heart results in spiritual blindness, not internal strength.

The apostle Peter is such a great example of someone who didn't let cynicism overtake him. Some like to point out his flaws and foolishness, but I think Peter demonstrates a soft heart. Let's take a look at one of his well-known moments in Matthew 14:26-33:

> When the disciples saw him walking on the lake, they were terrified. "It's a ghost," they said, and cried out in fear [so everyone's afraid]. But Jesus immediately said to them: "Take courage! It is I. Don't be afraid." "Lord, if it's you," Peter replied, "tell me to come to you on the water." "Come," Jesus said. Then Peter got down out of the boat, walked on the water and came toward Jesus. But when he saw the wind, he was [really] afraid and, beginning to sink, cried out, "Lord, save me!" Immediately Jesus reached out his hand and caught him. "You of little faith," he said, "why did you doubt?" And when they climbed into the boat, the wind died down. Then those who were in the boat [including Peter] worshiped him, saying, "Truly you are the Son of God."

Sure, Peter faltered. He was also the only one to get out of the boat. After he faltered, despite almost sinking into the sea, he bounced right back, declaring with the others, "Truly you are the

Son of God." His heart was soft enough to see past his own feelings of failures.

Keeping our hearts soft takes courage and clarity of purpose. Tolkien's *The Hobbit* demonstrates this well, helping us glimpse one of the tired heroes, Bilbo, moving forward, even while wrestling with fear:

> "Go back?" he thought. "No good at all! Go sideways? Impossible! Go forward? Only thing to do! On we go!" So up he got, and trotted along with his little sword held in front of him and one hand feeling the wall, and his heart all of a patter and a pitter.[4]

Cynicism is a false platform, a dressed-up and disguised form of insecurity. It is a fancy form of fear. Life is full of uncertainty. Uncertainty cannot be the dictator of our dreams and passions.

A RETURN TO HOPE

When I was twenty years old, I was faced with a predicament. It was almost Valentine's Day, my high school boyfriend and I broke up the year before, and I wasn't dating anyone. But I loved Valentine's Day. Looking out the window of my on-campus apartment as a single person on Valentine's Day, I remember thinking, *It seems like I have two options, neither of them great: (1) Hate and loathe the very existence of the holiday and eat chocolate, or (2) Feel sad all day, very aware of my singleness, totally excluded, and eat chocolate.*

I didn't like either option. I didn't want to hate the day, but I also didn't want to pretend the day didn't matter. I'm a romantic. What a hard tension it is to let ourselves be vulnerable by acknowledging our hopes and dreams, while also choosing to live the life we currently have with zest and fullness.

During this Valentine's Day predicament, I decided I'd approach the day with an assessment of my current loves, sort of like New Year's resolutions. I asked myself, *Who is the author of love? God. Okay, I'm going to celebrate him. What are my love goals for the next year? Okay, I'm going to figure out ways to care for my loved ones and care for myself better.* One way I would do this is take time to write a Valentine's Day card to people, including my future husband. And I told myself if I never got married, when I turn eighty years old, I'd offer them up in a bonfire.

Over a decade later, I celebrated my first Valentine's Day as a married person. My gift to Allen was a stack of Valentine's Day cards written over the past ten years. He didn't know about them. It was a lovely moment, handing him a red-ribbon-tied stack of cards at a low-lit restaurant, with tears wetting both of our cheeks.

We decided to open one card each night. Each time, we talked about where he was when I wrote it, how good God's timing is and how patient he is with us both. When Allen opened the first one, we both laughed at one part I wrote: "I want you to know that I am not waiting for my life to begin, for God is my life." Not all of the cards were so full of strength. There were a few written without much hope. The very last card I wrote before we met included a return to choosing hope: "Here I am. I won't wait for you, but I will hope for you, as I continue to dive forward in life." It takes courage to live with an open heart, in actual seasons of real uncertainty. Upon reflection, courage may sound romantic, but in the moment, it can be scary, lonely, and hard.

The other day, I asked one of my best friends, Jenn, what she thought about courage. She's seen her own share of hard. Here's what she said: "I think the people who are the most courageous (past and present) are those who know themselves and live out their God-given conviction, even if it looks different from their peers'. I think it's courageous to embrace how you are uniquely wired and do what God has placed on your heart to do."

Work calling challenges and complexities exist at every stage: college, post-college, a few years in, midlife, and even post-paid work or retirement. For example, Dennis contacted me about feeling burnout from a work calling after retirement. What he sees as his current work is caregiving and supporting family members and friends. Dennis said he truly believes we never leave the workplace; it's just our work roles that change. We are always meant to have a sense of purpose in what we do. Yet when the work doesn't seem like *work* to others, it can be harder to have clearer boundaries. This is where we need to think about how we are communicating about our work, to ourselves and to others. What we say impacts how others perceive us and guides our own perceptions. We must be careful with our calling communication.

THE WAY FORWARD

The stories that draw my attention, those that make me sit up and take notice, are not the ones with a perfect beginning, middle, and end. Nor are they dripping with painful sarcasm and grating discomfort from pushing the boundary lines so much that it's unclear who the hero or villain is.

The stories that hold my attention are those that help me see others better, with cinematic choices that make me take notice of everyday moments and people in fresh appreciation. The stories that draw my attention are ones with undeniable grit, where the characters do not succumb to the dark side, or if they do, they make a full return with an urgency to use their hard-earned wisdom for good. These stories are powerful and beautiful and hold a redemptive truth we were literally designed to realize.

My friends, we are not expected to know it all. But we are expected to keep learning. A healthy calling is a process. Burnout will always beckon like the sound of sharp-toothed sirens singing from shadowed oceans. Burnout can lure us into darkened spaces with continual doses of seemingly small compromises to our integrity and our boundaries, using toxic approaches like workaholism and idolization to take us further away from our original call.

A healthy calling does not deny the reality of burnout. Rather, it recognizes with awe the sacredness of relationship with the Caller, the community, and the calling itself. A healthy calling will flourish in the light of humility, freshly oiled and framed to help us orient and navigate our way through chaos and uncertain times.

A healthy calling is sustainable when we stay more concerned with our Caller than with our calling. It's not about perfecting our calling. It's about pursuing it in the healthiest manner possible. It's about protecting and practicing the real, true sentiment of "when I [fill in the blank with your calling], I feel God's pleasure."

GUIDING QUESTIONS

1. As you think about your work calling, what stories are you telling yourself these days?

   - What stories are you listening to? What we tell ourselves becomes what we believe. What we hear, day in and day out, becomes what we know.

   - Take a moment and reflect: What story are you telling yourself about your calling?

2. As it relates to your calling, what uncertainties are you facing right now?

   - How can you keep your heart soft and guard again cynicism?

3. What part of your calling story might you want to adjust moving forward?

  - Is there something you'd like to add or delete?

  - Share this with the Lord, the Author, the Creator, the Caller. Invite him to weave a new chapter.

  - Share this with a trusted friend. Keep yourself accountable. There may be times you want to give up. There may be times a new direction is need. Don't give up. Keep learning!

ORIENTING PRAYER

Oh perfect Love, thank you that you cast out all fear. Whatever fear is in me now, please take it out with your gentle hand. Oh great Caller, thank you for calling me to you. Help me to stay mindful of the last thing I heard you say to me. Oh heavenly Lord, thank you for equipping me with skills and passions and a desire to do good in your name. Please help me not to miss the signs of burnout in my own communication with others and with myself. Please forgive me for getting off track. Show me the way. Help me to hold all that you've given me with an open hand. Help me to walk humbly with you, oh God. Help me to keep learning. Guide me on, oh gracious Caller. Amen.

ACKNOWLEDGMENTS

To Stan Jantz, you are a visionary mentor who has the ability to help others mobilize their callings. Thank you for hearing my unspoken dream to write this book, even before I did. Thank you for believing in me, coaching me, and helping me learn the ropes. Your shepherding expertise and advocacy are kingdom treasures.

To my agent, Keely Boeving, thank you for seeing the potential of this book. I still remember our first phone call when you said to me, "You're the real deal." It felt like a movie moment crystalized in my living room filled with laundry and LEGO bricks. Thank you for helping me step into the world of book writing and not feel alone. Your heart to create positive and real change in this world gave me confidence to continue.

To my editor, Al Hsu, and the whole InterVarsity Press team, I had heard from others what a joy it was to work with you, but then I got to see it for myself. Al, from the moment I met you, I knew that you "got me." It is a rare skill indeed to provide authentically kind and truly clear feedback. You made the editing process feel fun—in the spirit of Mary Poppins' "In every job that must be done, there is an element of fun. You find the fun, and snap! The job's a game." I'd jump into a sidewalk chalk drawing with you any time!

To those who taught me what it means to be a person of integrity in my communication and learning: Debbie Pope, Bill Purcell, Todd Rendleman, Jeff Kerssen-Griep, Renee Heath, Christina Foust, Bryan Dik, Carrie Abbott, Deborah Taylor, and Shelly

Cunningham. You redeemed learning for me. You model an ethic of care, wisdom, good humor, intelligence, collaboration, and humanness that serves as a compass in the formation of my adulthood and continued growth in this season of my life. You've shown me how I hope to treat others in their own educational journeys.

To my students, you're on my heart so often. Before the start of each semester, I begin to pray for you. I remember the third year of my PhD program, walking on campus right before classes started, and watching freshmen holding orientation notebooks, trying to mask dazed looks on their faces, with family members trailing behind. I remember having a soft spark moment of wanting to walk alongside you and let you know that I see you, you're going to be okay, and you have what it takes to make a difference. I remember being a newly minted doctorate, full-time professor, feeling the full joy of being able to join you in your college process, to cheer you on with intentional guidance. It really is my hope that you feel seen, known, believed in, and equipped for what the Lord will call you to do. Thank you, thank you, thank you for letting me experience my work calling as your professor.

To my friends who rallied alongside me, letting me process the messy moments, and always offering me generosity of spirit. You know who you are! Special shout out to Carolyn Kim for reminding me on a weekly basis that I can do this, Jenn Branstetter for a longevity of faithful friendship, Bekah Buchterkirchen and Jessica Journeay for asking me to coffee and to mentor you in my first year as a professor and for becoming the dearest of friends in the following years, and Arielle Leonard Hodges as my anchoring coffee shop buddy in the final year of this book writing process. Emotionally safe friendships are rare.

To my Cutler tribe, thank you for modeling a life-learning mentality, resilience, grit, creativity, beauty, compassion, generosity, familial inclusiveness to all, and tenacious strength.

To my parents, Bill and Johanna, I know the Lord because of you. I know what love looks like because of you. I know what safety feels like because of you. I know what faithfulness means because of you. I know how to parent well because of you. There will never be enough space to explain how grateful I am to be your daughter and friend.

To my husband, Allen, and son, Asher, you are my home. Allen, thank you for always helping me pursue my dreams and never asking me to make them (or me) smaller. Thank you for being a true partner and my very best friend. I'm so grateful the Lord saved us for each other. And, Asher, although I have been quite familiar with the concept of calling, experiencing the new calling of being your mom is a gift that leaves me speechless. The Lord is so kind, so miraculous in his ways, to let me be your mom. Not only do I adore you, I also really like you. My dear ones, I love forever and always.

To my Lord, I am humbled by the touch of your hand on my life and your felt presence from the time I can remember. Thank you for teaching me about your love and faithfulness, thank you for pursuing me, being patient with me, forgiving me, being bigger than my fears and failures, opening doors that felt like walls, and creating new pathways when I couldn't see any. You are my anchor, my hope, my source. Thank you for allowing me to experience work and relationships as a calling. May it all be for your glory.

NOTES

INTRODUCTION: THE PATH TO BURNOUT AND WHY IT MATTERS

[1] Ryan Duffy and Bryan Dik, "Research on Calling: What Have We Learned and Where Are We Going?," *Journal of Vocational Behavior*, 83 (2013): 428-36.

[2] Brenda L Berkelaar and Patrice M. Buzzanell, "Bait and Switch or Double-Edged Sword? The (Sometimes) Failed Promises of Calling," *Human Relations*, 68, no. 1 (May 2015): 157-78, doi: 10.1177/0018726714526265.

[3] Michele W. Gazica and Paul E. Spector, "A Comparison of Individuals with Unanswered Callings to Those with No Calling At All," *Journal of Vocational Behavior*, 91 (2015): 1-10, http://dx.doi.org/10.1016/j.jvb.2015.08.008.

[4] K. A. Molloy, B. J. Dick, D. E. Davis, and R. D. Duffy, "Work Calling and Humility: Framing for Job Idolization, Workaholism, and Exploitation," *Journal of Management, Spirituality, and Religion*, 16, no. 5 (2019): 428-44, doi: 10.1080/14766086.2019.1657489.

[5] Frederick Buechner, *Wishful Thinking: A Theological ABC* (San Francisco, CA: HarperSanFrancisco, 1993), 118-19.

[6] Angela Duckworth, *Grit: The Power of Passion and Perseverance* (New York: Scribner Book Company, 2006); Greg McKeown, *Essentialism: The Disciplined Pursuit of Less* (New York: Crown Business, 2014).

[7] Molloy, Dik, Davis, and Duffy, "Work Calling and Humility."

1. THE TOXIC RELATIONSHIP BETWEEN BURNOUT AND CALLING

[1] *Chariots of Fire*, directed by Hugh Hudson (London: Allied Stars Ltd, Enigma Productions, 1981).

[2] InterVarsity Press editor Al Hsu addresses this distinction in what he calls "The Dilbertization of Work," Al Hsu, "The Dilbertization of Work," https://ifl.web.baylor.edu/sites/g/files/ecbvkj771/files/2023-02/vocationarticlehsu.pdf. Organizational psychologist Adam Grant's work on *flow* received quite a bit of attention during the height of the Covid-19 pandemic, where he further examined the distinction of "meh" work and work that feels like "flow." The term

flow was originally coined by Mihaly Csikszentmihalyi, *Flow* (New York: HarperPerennial, 1990).

3 G. Cheney, T. E. Zorn, S. Planalp, and D. J. Lair, "Meaningful Work and Personal/Social Well-Being: Organizational Communication Engages the Meanings of Work," *Communication Yearbook*, 32 (2008), 137-85, www.icahdq.org/publications/commyearbook.asp.

4 J. M. Berg, A. M. Grant, and V. Johnson, "When Callings are Calling: Crafting Work and Leisure in Pursuit of Unanswered Occupational Callings," *Organization Science*, 21 (2010): 973–94, doi:10.1287/orsc.1090.0497; see also Indeed Editorial Team, "How Often Do People Change Careers?," Indeed, February 13, 2024, www.indeed.com/career-advice/starting-new-job/how-often-do-people-change-careers.

5 Dan J. Lair, Suchitra Shenoy, John McClellan, and Tammy McGuire, "The Politics of Meaning/ful Work: Navigating the Tensions of Narcissism and Condescension While Finding Meaning at Work," *Management Communication Quarterly*, 22, no. 1 (2008), 172-78, doi: 10.1177/0893318908318263.

6 Robin Patric Clair, Megan McConnell, Stephanie Bell, Kyle Hackbarth, and Stephanie Mathes, *Why Work: The Perceptions of a "Real Job" and the Rhetoric of Work Through the Ages* (West Lafayette, IN: Purdue University Press, 2008); see also Robin Patric Clair, "The Political Nature of the Colloquialism, 'a Real Job': Implications for Organizational Socialization," *Communication Monographs*, 63 (1996), 249–67, doi:10.1080/03637759609376392.

7 Bryan J. Dik and Ryan D. Duffy, *Make Your Job a Calling* (West Conshohocken, PA: Templeton Press, 2012).

8 For our purposes, when I refer to the Caller, I'm talking about God. However, I do want to point out that among my interviews with participants who identify with a sense of calling, some people have referred to their caller as the universe, an inner voice, and even their guitar or paint brush. This language is not something that exists only in Christian circles. I suggest it's because as a relational being, God literally designed us to desire communication with him and respond to his call—whether we know it's him calling or not. This is another reason why understanding our work callings is not just an individual process; it is also missional.

9 John Mark Comer, *Practicing the Way: Be with Jesus, Become Like Him, Do as He Did* (Colorado Springs, CO: Waterbrook, 2024), xii.

10 Os Guinness, *The Call: Finding and Fulfilling God's Purpose for Your Life* (Nashville, TN: Thomas Nelson, 2018), 4.

11 Dik and Duffy, *Make Your Job a Calling*.

[12] K. A. Molloy and R. G. Heath, "Bridge Discourses and Organizational Ideologies: Managing Spiritual and Secular Communication in a Faith-Based, Nonprofit Organization," *International Journal of Business Communication*, 51 (2014), 15, doi: 10.1177/2329488414525451.

[13] Susan L. Maros, *Calling in Context* (Downers Grove, IL: InterVarsity Press, 2022).

[14] K. Arianna Molloy and Christina R. Foust, "Work Calling: Exploring the Communicative Intersections of Meaningful Work and Organizational Spirituality," *Journal of Communication Studies*, 67, no. 3 (2016): 1-20, doi: 10.1080/10510974.2016.114875.

[15] J. Steward Bunderson and Jeffery A. Thompson, "The Call of the Wild: Zookeepers, Callings, and the Double-Edged Sword of Deeply Meaningful Work," *Administrative Science Quarterly*, 54, no. 1 (2009): 32-57, doi: 10.2189/asqu.2009.54.1.32.

2. CHRONIC STRESS AND THE DEADLY DUO OF WORKAHOLISM AND JOB IDOLIZATION

[1] Bessel van der Kolk, *The Body Keeps the Score: Brain, Mind, and Body in the Healing of Trauma* (New York: Viking, 2014).

[2] Wendy L. Patrick, "Stretch for Success: How Posture Can Improve Self-Esteem," *Psychology Today*, February 11, 2021, www.psychologytoday.com/us/blog/why-bad-looks-good/202102/stretch-success-how-posture-can-improve-self-esteem.

[3] Peter A. Andersen, *Nonverbal Communication: Forms and Functions*, 2nd ed. (Long Grove, Il: Waveland Press, 2008); see also N. Schneiderman, G. Ironson, and S. D. Siegel, "Stress And Health: Psychological, Behavioral, and Biological Determinants," *Annual Review of Clinical Psychology*, 1 (2005), 607–28, https://doi.org/10.1146/annurev.clinpsy.1.102803.144141.

[4] Anderson, *Nonverbal Communication*.

[5] Andrew Murray, *Humility: The Journey Toward Holiness* (Bloomington, MN: Bethany House Publishers, 2001).

[6] Richard J. Foster, *Prayer: Finding Your Heart's True Home* (San Francisco: HarperOne, 2002).

[7] Greg McKeown, *Essentialism: The Disciplined Pursuit of Less* (New York: Crown Currency, 2014).

[8] "Top 10 Most Popular TED Talks of All Time," LinkedIn, published April 28, 2023, www.linkedin.com/pulse/top-10-most-popular-ted-talks-all-time-jignen-p-sales-leader-/.

[9] Simon Sinek, *Start with Why: How Great Leaders Inspire Everyone to Take Action* (New York: Penguin Group, 2011).

3. THE THREE Cs IN CALLING'S RELATIONAL CORE

[1] *Chariots of Fire*, directed by Hugh Hudson (London: Allied Stars Ltd, Enigma Productions, 1981).

[2] Justin Earley, *The Common Rule: Habits of Purpose in an Age of Distraction* (Downers Grove, IL: InterVarsity Press, 2019).

[3] R. G. Heath, "Rethinking Community Collaboration Through a Dialogic Lens: Creativity, Democracy, and Diversity in Community Organizing," *Management Communication Quarterly*, 21 (2007), 145-71, doi: 10.1177/0893318907306032; see also T. Kuhn, "Negotiating Boundaries Between Scholars and Practitioners: Knowledge, Networks, and Communities of Practice," *Management Communication Quarterly*, 16 (2002), 106-12, doi: 10.1177/089331890216100.

[4] J. M. Berg, A. M. Grant, and V. Johnson, "When Callings Are Calling: Crafting Work and Leisure in Pursuit of Unanswered Occupational Callings," *Organization Science*, 21 (2010): 973-94, doi:10.1287/orsc.1090.0497.

[5] Sean Manning, "Work Migration: The Rise of Remote Working and You," *Forbes*, January 30, 2024, www.forbes.com/sites/forbesbusinesscouncil/2024/01/30/work-migration-the-rise-of-remote-working-and-you/?sh=5f03f4059076; see also Tim Smart, "Remote Work Has Radically Changed the Economy—and It's Here to Stay," *U. S. News*, January 25, 2024, www.usnews.com/news/economy/articles/2024-01-25/remote-work-has-radically-changed-the-economy-and-its-here-to-stay.

[6] Robin Patric Clair, Megan McConnell, Stephanie Bell, Kyle Hackbarth, and Stephanie Mathes, *Why Work: The Perceptions of a "Real Job" and the Rhetoric of Work Through the Ages* (West Lafayette, IN: Purdue University Press, 2008); see also Robin Patric Clair, "The Political Nature of the Colloquialism, 'a Real Job': Implications for Organizational Socialization," *Communication Monographs*, 63 (1996), 249–67, doi:10.1080/03637759609376392.

[7] Berg, Grant, and Johnson, "When Callings Are Calling."

[8] I have seen a few rare organizations who pull off the family metaphor well. In these instances, the leader cares for their organizational members with a kind of familial valuing evident in clear commitment to the well-being and development of each person. It's not impossible to approach work this way, but it can be especially complicated. One particular problem with the family metaphor is we don't fire family.

[9] Stanley Deetz, *Transforming Communication, Transforming Business: Building Responsive and Responsible Workplaces* (Cresskill, NJ: Hampton Press, 1995); see also R. G. Heath, "Rethinking Community Collaboration Through a Dialogic Lens: Creativity, Democracy, and Diversity in Community Organizing," *Management Communication Quarterly* 21 (2007), 145-71, doi: 10.1177 /0893318907306032.

[10] Marian Wright Edelman, *Families in Peril: An Agenda for Social Change* (Boston: Harvard University Press, 1989).

[11] Kathleen J. Krone, Paul Schrodt, and Erika L. Kirby, "Structuration Theory: Promising Directions for Family Communication Research," in *Engaging Theories in Family Communication: Multiple Perspectives* (New York: SAGE Publications, 2006), 107, 293-308, https://doi.org/10.4135/9781452204420.

[12] Robin Patric Clair, "The Political Nature of the Colloquialism, 'a Real Job': Implications for Organizational Socialization," *Communication Monographs*, 63 (1996), 249–67, doi:10.1080/03637759609376392.

[13] Virginia Sánchez Sánchez, "'Dando las Gracias a Mis Papás': Analyzing the Enactment of Callings across Generations of Latinx Immigrants," *Journal of Communication* 71, no. 6 (September 2021): 976–1000, https://doi.org /10.1093/joc/jqab037.

[14] Bryan J. Dik and Ryan D. Duffy, *Make Your Job a Calling* (West Conshohocken, PA: Templeton Press, 2012).

4. THE MISUNDERSTOOD AND UNDERREPRESENTED ROLE OF HUMILITY

[1] Some of the material from this chapter originated in a talk I gave at Biola University Chapel, available on YouTube, "Arianna Molloy: What It Means to Walk Humbly with Your God," February 3, 2020, https://youtu.be/CbzVFiG4Fzc?si =V4TcUPlf3g1WDGq0.

[2] For a great understanding of burnout being like a tunnel, see Emily Nagoski and Amelia Nagoski, *Burnout: The Secret to Unlocking the Stress Cycle* (New York: Ballantine Books, 2020).

[3] See Dennis R. Edwards, *Humility Illuminated: The Biblical Path Back to Christian Character* (Downers Grove, IL: InterVarsity Press, 2023); Andrew Murray, *Humility: The Journey Toward Holiness* (Minneapolis, MN: Bethany House, 2001); and D. E. Davis, E. L. Worthington Jr., and J. N. Hook, "Humility: Review of Measurement Strategies and Conceptualization as Personality Judgment," *The Journal of Positive Psychology*, 5 (2010): 243-52, http://dx.doi .org/10.1080/17439761003791672.

Also see John Dickson, *Humilitas: A Lost Key to Life, Love, and Leadership* (Grand Rapids, MI: Zondervan, 2011); Jane Foulcher, *Reclaiming Humility: Four Studies in the Monastic Tradition* (Piffard, NY: Cistercian Publications, 2015); J. L. Kvanvig, "Intellectual Humility: Lessons from the Preface Paradox," *Res Philosophica* 93 (2016): 509-32, doi:10.11612/resphil.2016.93.3.8; B. P. Owens, M. D. Johnson, and T. R. Mitchell, "Expressed Humility in Organizations: Implications for Performance, Teams, and Leadership," *Organization Science*, 24 (2013): 1517-38, doi:10.1287/orsc.1120.0795; R. C. Roberts, "Humility and Epistemic Goods (with W. Jay Wood)," in *Intellectual Virtue: Perspectives from Ethics and Epistemology*, eds. Michael DePaul and Linda Zagzebski (Oxford: Oxford University Press, 2003), 257-79; J. P. Tangney, "Humility: Theoretical Perspectives, Empirical, Findings, and Directions for Future Research," *Journal of Social Clinical Psychology* 19 (2000): 70-82, doi: 10.1521/jscp.2000.19.1.70; and K. A. Molloy, B. J. Dick, D. E. Davis, and R. D. Duffy, "Work Calling and Humility: Framing for Job Idolization, Workaholism, and Exploitation," *Journal of Management, Spirituality, and Religion* 16 (2019): 428-44, doi: 10.1080/14766086.2019.1657489.

[4] C. S. Lewis, *Mere Christianity* (San Francisco: HarperSanFrancisco, 2009).

[5] Jane Foulcher, *Reclaiming Humility: Four Studies in the Monastic Tradition* (Collegeville, MN: Liturgical Press, 2015), 29.

[6] Jim Collins, *Good to Great: Why Some Companies Make the Leap While Other Don't* (New York: HarperBusiness, 2001); Patrick Lencioni, *The Ideal Team Player: How to Recognize and Cultivate the Three Essential Virtues* (Hoboken, NJ: Jossey-Bass, 2016).

[7] Dennis Edwards, *Humility Illuminated: The Biblical Path Back to Christian Character* (Downers Grove, IL: IVP Academic, 2023).

[8] James Clear, *Atomic Habits: Tiny Changes, Remarkable Results: An Easy and Proven Way to Build Good Habits and Break Bad Ones* (New York: Generic, 2021).

[9] James Clear, "You do not rise . . . ," jamesclear.com, accessed May 1, 2024, https://jamesclear.com/quotes/you-do-not-rise-to-the-level-of-your-goals-you-fall-to-the-level-of-your-systems.

5. PRACTICING HEALTHY HUMILITY

[1] John Dickson, *Humilitas: A Lost Key to Life, Love, and Leadership* (Grand Rapids, MI: Zondervan, 2011).

[2] Carol S. Dweck, *Mindset: The Psychology of Success* (New York: Ballantine Books, 2007).

[3] Charles E. Hummel, *Tyranny of the Urgent* (Downers Grove, IL: InterVarsity Press, 1994).

[4] *Finding Nemo*, directed by Andrew Stanton (Los Angeles: Walt Disney Pictures, 2003).

[5] "The Sabbath Practice," Practicing the Way, accessed May 1, 2024, www .practicingtheway.org/sabbath; "How Do You Protect Your Rest and Sabbath Time?," Lausanne Movement, May 26, 2022, https://lausanne.org/about /blog/how-do-you-protect-your-rest-and-sabbath-time.

6. BOUNDARY SHAMING AND BOUNDARY RESILIENCE

[1] Soren Kierkegaard, *Provocations: Spiritual Writings of Kierkegaard* (Walden, NY: Bruderhof, 2002), 187.

[2] Brie W. Reynolds, "FlexJobs, Mental Health America Survey: Mental Health in the Workplace," FlexJobs, August 21, 2020, www.flexjobs.com/blog/post /flexjobs-mha-mental-health-workplace-pandemic/.

[3] Jennifer Moss, *The Burnout Epidemic: The Rise of Chronic Stress and How We Can Fix It* (Boston, MA: Harvard Business Review Press, 2021); "Job Unhappiness Is at a Staggering All-Time High, According to Gallup," CNBC, August 12, 2022, www.cnbc.com/2022/08/12/job-unhappiness-is-at-a-staggering-all -time-high-according-to-gallup.html.

[4] Moss, *The Burnout Epidemic.*

[5] Brené Brown, "The Power of Vulnerability," TEDx Houston, TED video, 20:02, www.ted.com/talks/brene_brown_the_power_of_vulnerability.

[6] "What is Chronic Shame?," PsychCentral, April 8, 2022, https://psychcentral .com/depression/depression-or-chronic-shame.

[7] Jeremy Sutton, "Shame Resilience Theory: Advice From Brené Brown," Positive Psychology, June 14, 2017, https://positivepsychology.com/shame-resilience -theory/.

[8] Douglas J. Rumford, "How to Say No Graciously," *Christianity Today*, accessed May 1, 2024, www.christianitytoday.com/pastors/1982/fall/saynograciously .html.

[9] For more information, see Cloud-Townsend Resources, accessed May 1, 2024, www.cloudtownsend.com.

[10] Henry Cloud and John S. Townsend, *Boundaries: When to Say Yes, When to Say No to Take Control of Your Life* (Grand Rapids, MI: Zondervan, 2017).

[11] Arielle Leonard, Arianna Molloy, Bekah Buchterkichen, Jessica Journeay, and Tess Buckly, "Renewal in a Culture of Accepted Burnout: Transforming from

Boundary Shaming to Boundary (Re)Claiming," Research Panel Presentation, National Communication Association Conference, Seattle, WA, 2021.

[12] Te-Li Lau, *Defending Shame: It's Formative Power in Paul's Letters* (Grand Rapids, MI: Baker Academic, 2020).

[13] Heather Thompson Day, "TikTok Therapy: Red Flag or Green Flag," with Kobe Campbell, August 24, 2023, on *Viral Jesus* podcast, www.boomplay.com /episode/5033150?srModel=COPYLINK&srList=WEB.

7. OIL AND FRAMES

[1] Leslie Barrie, "11 Best and Worst Oils for Your Health," Everyday Health, February 14, 2023, www.everydayhealth.com/news/best-worst-oils-health/.

[2] "What the Bible Says About Oil as Symbol," Bible Tools, accessed May 1, 2024, www.bibletools.org/index.cfm/fuseaction/topical.show/RTD/cgg/ID/1107 /Oil-as-Symbol.htm.

[3] "17 Reasons Humility Will Help You Get Ahead," *Forbes*, October 17, 2017, www.forbes.com/sites/forbescoachescouncil/2017/10/17/17-reasons -humility-will-help-you-get-ahead/?sh=4d7bde8fac3a; Tyrone Sgambati, "Five Reasons Why Intellectual Humility Is Good for You," *Greater Good Magazine*, February 16, 2022, https://greatergood.berkeley.edu/article/item /five_reasons_why_intellectual_humility_is_good_for_you.

[4] Don E. Davis, Everett L. Worthington, and Joshua N. Hook, "Humility: Review of Measurement Strategies and Conceptualization as Personality Judgment," *The Journal of Positive Psychology* 5, no. 4 (July 2010): 243-52, http://dx.doi .org/10.1080/17439761003791672.

[5] Emily Nagoski and Amelia Nagoski, *Burnout: The Secret to Unlocking the Stress Cycle* (New York: Random House, 2020).

[6] Gail Fairhurst, "Reframing the Art of Framing: Problems and Prospects for Leadership," *Leadership* 1, no. 2 (2005): 165-85, doi:10.1177 /1742715005051857; Gail Fairhurst and Robert Sarr, *The Art of Framing: Managing the Language of Leadership* (San Francisco: Jossey-Bass, 1996); J. M. Smith, C. Arendt, J. B. Lahman, G. N. Settle, and A. Duff, "Framing the Work of Art: Spirituality and Career Discourse in the Nonprofit Arts Sector," *Communication Studies* 57, (2006): 25-46, doi:10.1080//10510970500481672.

[7] CeCe Winans, Kyle Lee, Dwan Hill, and Mitch Wong, "Believe For It," *Believe For It* (Puresprings Gospel and Fair Trade Services, 2021).

8. THE WAY FORWARD

[1] Joseph A. Cannon, "The Gospel in Words: Word of the Week: 'Remember'," Deseret News, March 27, 2008, www.deseret.com/2008/3/27/20078709/the

-gospel-in-words-word-of-the-week-remember#:~:text=It%20would%20be
%20difficult%20to,mind%20or%20to%20be%20mindful.

[2] *A League of Their Own*, directed by Penny Marshall (Culver City, CA: Columbia
Pictures, 1992).

[3] Shel Silverstein, *The Giving Tree* (New York: HarperCollins, 2006).

[4] J. R. R. Tolkien, *The Hobbit* (Boston: Mariners Books, 2012), 66.